THEATRE LIBRARY ASSOCIATION

The Theatre Library Association is a non-profit organization established in 1937 to advance the interests of all those involved in collecting and preserving performing arts materials and in utilizing those materials for purpose of scholarship. The membership is international and includes public and private institutions, as well as librarians, archivists, curators, conservators, private collectors, historians, teachers, designers, actors, writers, and all other interested persons. The Theatre Library Association meets annually to conduct its business in the fall of each year. It presents a day of conferences and programs during the annual meeting of the American Library Association, and frequently cooperates with other professional and scholarly organizations in the sponsorship of symposia, events and publications.

The Theatre Library Association publishes Broadside, *a quarterly newsletter,* Performing Arts Resources, *an annual journal, and occasional conference compendia.*

It is governed by a constitution which provides for a board of directors elected by the membership and officers elected by the board.

THE THEATRE LIBRARY
ASSOCIATION BOOK AWARDS

Two awards are presented annually for books of unusual merit and distinction in the fields served by the Association.

The George Freedley Award, *established in 1968, honors work in the field of theatre published in the United States. Only books with subjects related to live performance will be considered. They may be biography, history or criticism.*

The Theatre Library Association Award, *established in 1973, honors a book published in the United States in the field of recorded performance, which includes motion pictures, radio and television.*

Works ineligible for both awards are textbooks; anthologies; collections of essays previously published in other sources; reprints; works on dance, ballet and opera; plays and similar dramatic works. Translations of significant works, other than play texts, will be considered. Entries will be judged on the basis of scholarship, readability and general contribution of knowledge to the fields served by the Association. No galley sheets or proofs will be accepted. Books nominated for awards must be published in the calendar year prior to the presentation of the awards and must be received no later than March 1 of the year following publication.

Nominations are to be submitted in writing to the Chair, Book Awards Committee, in care of the Theatre Library Association, 111 Amsterdam Avenue, New York, N.Y. 10023.

PERFORMING ARTS RESOURCES, the annual publication of the Theatre Library Association, is designed to gather and disseminate scholarly articles dealing with location of resource materials relating to theatre, film, television, radio, video and popular entertainments; descriptions, listings, or evaluations of the contents of such collections, whether public or private; and monographs of previously unpublished original source material.

Please submit query letter only. All manuscripts must be typed cleanly on one side only, double-spaced, and adhering to the style and method described in the MLA Style Sheet, Second Edition. Discs will not be accepted. Please include a list of appropriate illustrative material; black-and-white photographs and line cuts will be used at the discretion of the editor.

Please send all correspondence to:

Performing Arts Resources
c/o Theatre Library Association
111 Amsterdam Avenue/PARC
New York, New York 10023

PERFORMING ARTS RESOURCES

Edited by
Barbara Naomi Cohen-Stratyner

VOLUME FOURTEEN

PERFORMANCES IN PERIODICALS

Published by the Theatre Library Association

The Library of Congress catalogued this serial as follows:
Performing Arts Resources
    Vols. for 1974 – issued by the Theatre Library Association
    ISSN 0360-3814
1. Performing arts – Library resources – United States – Periodicals
I. Theatre Library Association
Z6935.P46   016.7902'08   75-646287
ISBN   0-932610-11-0

Produced by Sans Serif, Inc. Ann Arbor, Michigan
Manufactured in the United States of America
This serial is printed on acid-free paper.

TABLE OF CONTENTS

Illustrations reproduced through the courtesy of The Margaret
Woodbury Strong Museum, Rochester, New York; the Shubert
Archive; and The New York Public Library.

FROM THE EDITOR

Performing Arts Resources is published annually by the Theatre Library Association to make available reference materials to scholars, curators, and the staffs of arts and general-readership libraries. In our past fourteen volumes, authors have announced major discoveries, presented new translations and revealed unearthed treasures in all of the performing and broadcast arts.

Volume Fourteen, which focuses on information in periodicals from the nineteenth and early twentieth century, is dedicated to the twin themes of availability and serendipity. These magazines, from the children's monthlies that Florence Smith scoured for Charades texts to the film studio house organs in which Julie Malnig and I found information on exhibition ballroom dance and couture, are gradually becomming more available in microform. The theatrical trade papers analyzed by Stephen M. Vallillo are completely microfilmed while the one discussed by Maryann Chach can be seen in partial runs. The technical sides of the arts are presented in two articles that focus on new inventions as they were interpreted to the American public. Jack McCullough brings us a treasure trove of descriptions and analyses on theatre from technical magazines of the nineteenth century. Sara Velez traces the announcements, publicizing and industry of recorded sound from the very beginning in her international bibliography of periodicals from 1880 to 1929.

The research that created the articles in this volume was inspired by biographies, by exhibitions and, in one case, by chance. The scholarship that can be inspired by the material that *Performing Arts Resources* presents in this volume can lead readers into paths of their own that cross boundaries of catagorization.

INTRODUCING PARLOR THEATRICALS TO THE AMERICAN HOME

by Florence C. Smith

Giving performances before an audience of family and friends was an important part of socializing for Americans in the last half of the nineteenth century. Amateur performances might be impromptu or carefully planned, and they took many forms. A number of periodicals from this period offer intriguing information about pantomimes, charades, recitations, and tableaux – unfamiliar forms of dramatic entertainment to many modern Americans.

In a sense, however, parlor theatricals need no introduction. The word "theatrical" brings visions of earnest but unpolished actors, dressed in costume, entertaining a small audience with exaggerated actions and dialogue in their "acting" voices. The word "parlor" sets the stage for these theatricals. Parlors belong to Victorian houses and bring to mind a special room, or maybe two adjoining rooms, where families and friends gathered for social occasions. As Katherine Grier has so ably described in her book *Culture and Comfort: People, Parlors, and Upholstery, 1850-1930*, this parlor "was used for purposes of social ceremony – the place in which calls and social visits by friends were received and the setting for entertainments such as tea parties and musicales."[1]

FLORENCE SMITH is the lead educator for adult programs at the Strong Museum in Rochester, New York. A graduate of Wellesley College and a candidate for an M.A. in American history, she has served as a part of the exhibit team for the *Culture and Comfort: People, Parlors and Upholstery, 1850-1930*, at the Strong Museum in September 1988. As educator for the four-part exhibit, *Americans at Play*, she has worked on the script and exhibition materials for *Armchair Adventures and Parlor Pursuits, 1880-1920*, which includes a section of parlor performance.

Parlors had numerous sofas and chairs and were decorated with the family's best furnishings, which made them suitable for an audience. The floors were carpeted, the windows draped, and, best of all, the entryway was often festooned with lambrequins and portieres, creating an ideal proscenium for whatever went on within the frame. In America, Grier has noted, "when portieres became a furnishing convention in the 1880s, they also reflected the continuing interest ordinary consumers had in maintaining some sense of the theatrical, cultured facade of the parlor."[2]

Parlor theatricals also evoke a specific period of time in American social history, beginning in the late 1850s. Earlier American attitudes toward the use of leisure time restricted time spent on activities considered frivolous, time-consuming, and corrupting, including theater in any form. Advice literature reinforced these feelings: in 1858, domestic adviser Catharine Beecher warned that "the only legitimate object of amusements is to prepare mind and body for the proper discharge of duty."[3] Even amusements that were not wrong in themselves but tempted an individual to stray from his duties were to be avoided. "So with theatres," Beecher wrote, "The enacting of characters, and the amusement thus afforded, in itself may be harmless; and possibly, in certain cases, might be useful: but experience has shown so many evils to result from this source, that it is deemed wrong to patronize it."[4]

It was in this same decade of the 1850s that a significant number of periodicals began to be available to the American public. Frank Luther Mott's comprehensive five-volume work, *A History of American Magazines*, gives detailed information about the founding, career spans, and contents of magazines from 1741 to 1930. Mott describes a surge of literary periodicals in the 1850s that brought serialized English novels, opinion, information, and advice right into the American home.

At least thirty periodicals in the period between 1850 and 1865 were aimed at women and the home or the family.[5] These included the enduring *Godey's* magazines, first published in 1830 in Philadelphia as the *Lady's Book*, and *Peterson's Magazine*, founded in 1842. *Godey's Lady's Book and Magazine*, as it came to be known in 1854, reached its circulation apex just before the Civil War,[6] after which it was overshadowed by *Peterson's Magazine*, which claimed in 1866 to have the largest circulation of any periodical for ladies in the United States.[7]

In order to be successful, the contents of these publications needed to be acceptable to those who bought and read them. A study of some of the periodicals aimed at women and children gives a sense of when attitudes toward the theater relaxed enough to allow Americans to bring "theater" into their homes. Some early nineteenth-century magazines, such as the *Boston Magazine* and the *American Monthly* in New York City, paid attention to public theater.[8] But the disapproving attitude expressed by Catharine Beecher seems to have prevailed into the 1850s.

One of the earliest and most significant indications of a changing attitude was a December 1854 article in *Godey's Lady's Book and Magazine* entitled "Charades in Action." The article indicated that this magazine was introducing a new activity to Americans. It described the activity as "acting-charades," or "little games," "excuses for locomotion" borrowed from the French.[9] Old people, the article claimed, lay aside their dignity and excused themselves for doing so by saying that they liked to see young people enjoy themselves. "Lately, the game has been introduced into the drawing-rooms in this country and has become very popular."[10]

The directions for these charades instructed the group of players to divide into two groups, one of which decided upon a word divisible into two parts. These two parts and then the whole word were to be acted out "as puzzlingly as possible in dumb show."[11] If, at the end of the acting, the other half of the group could guess the word, they in turn performed. If not, the first group continued by acting out another word.

The word "courtship" was used to illustrate how this game should be played. The first act illustrated the word "court," by depicting the activities taking place at a court of justice. The second act described the word "ship" by depicting the behavior of a ship's captain and his passengers during a storm. The final act portrayed the entire word in a scene that included a lover hiding under the dining table and his reconciliation with his beloved's gout-ridden father. All this was to be acted silently. The article included directions for acting out a charade, which were rarely included in other articles published after this one. Usually, the charades and other dramas that appeared in the next few decades were simply scripts and casts of characters.

Godey's Lady's Book and Magazine took care in this early article to make several suggestions, including "the proper delivery of the gestures in the pantomime reading of the parts"[12] and a detailed "code of expressions" with readily recognizable positions and actions for love, rage, despair, hope, disdain, giving a blessing, and weeping. Scenery and costumes were necessary, but the article warned the hostess for this evening's entertainment that everything would be hastily prepared. "No expense should be spared, and every sacrifice be made, even though the incidents of the piece should include the upsetting of a tray of tea things, or the blacking of all the young ladies' faces."[13]

After introducing this new form of amusement to American homes in 1854, *Godey's* only occasionally printed additional articles about domestic drama. The February issue in 1860 offered a four-page script for a charade of the word "masterpiece."

In June of 1860, however, the first in a series of "Ella Moore's Letters from the City" appeared and continued through November, giving an "account of our various ways of passing the evenings this winter."[14] The first letter described another new amusement, a tableau party for the members of the household whom this author was visiting and for their friends. Held in the evening in the double parlor, these tableaux or stage pictures were posed by some of the guests, using costumes and props to create a well-known scene from history or popular literature for the other guests to view, admire, and identify. The author described the decorations and several kinds of curtains needed for the presentation of a tableau and gave a detailed description of how each guest played his part in scenes entitled "The Bleeding Nun," the ballroom scene from "Cinderella," and "The Sorceress."[15] The July 1860 issue continued with descriptions of four more tableaux— "Grandmother's Trunk," "The Dying Brigand," "Second Sight," and "The Intercepted Letter."[16]

The second letter, published in August, gave an account of an evening of charades. As in the 1854 article, words were acted out in their separate parts and then as a whole, but the rule about silent acting had changed. The description for the words that were presented for this evening entertainment included words to be spoken. The five charades were for the words "innocent," "patchwork," "songstress," "courtship," and "dramatic."[17] This version of courtship was different from the 1854 version.

The third letter also described impromptu charades, using proverbs such as "All's well that ends well" instead of single words. Again, words were to be spoken as these proverbs were acted out. The proverb "It never rains but pours" presented a gentleman worrying aloud about unpaid bills, the landlady knocking on the door to demand her rent, dishes being broken, and a canceled engagement for taking a young lady to the opera for lack of money. The tide was turned in the final scene when this same young lady turned out to be an heiress.[18]

The last letter in the October and November issues for 1860 described a birthday party in which guests participated in "moving tableaux." Four scenes were acted out, again with words as well as actions, including a scene from Joan of Arc's trial. The letter recommended a "full dress rehearsal" because, although the scenes "are very effective and entertaining," if they were "poorly rendered, they would be very wearisome."[19] The random appearance of other articles about parlor theatricals in subsequent issues of *Godey's* makes them difficult to find, but the researcher will be rewarded with a number of scripts for acting charades. In January, March, and May of 1870, scripts appeared for "Frenchman," "Checkmate," and "Waterfall."[20] The February 1873 issue offered a charade in four parts for "Window-Pane," using the words "wind," "oh!," and "pain" before dramatizing the whole word.[21] In October of the same year, the proverb "There are none so blind as those who will not see" was the subject for a charade script.[22]

The fine line between a charade that acts out a four-syllable word with four scenes connected by the same plot and a play was crossed in a script published in March and April of 1885. The script "Dining-Room Charade" was written by Mrs. V. Sheffey Haller, and is fifteen-pages long.[23] Settings, the cast of more than twenty characters, and acting directions for this humorous tale of spoiled fish and secret love was presented in the form of a play and required much more preparation and rehearsal than the "courtship" charade described in *Godey's* thirty-one years earlier. By the 1880s, the subject matter for these amateur dramas continued to concern domestic issues, but American periodicals were offering much more elaborate dramatizations.

Peterson's Magazine also published some domestic drama. In the January 1860 issue, S. Annie Frost offered a charade for "Man-age," which was reprinted from her book, an indication that this form of amusement was popular enough to warrent special publications in book form.[24] Another charade for the word "antidote" appeared in March 1862.[25] The extension of parlor theatricals to entertainment for young people is illustrated in an 1885 frontispiece in *Peterson's* entitled "Dressed for the Charade," which shows two children in costume.[26]

Indeed, drama for children had been published in several periodicals intended for young readers since the 1860s. As early as 1858, at least some Americans had relaxed their attitude towards theater enough to recommend dramatic entertainment for young people in the safety of the home environment. *Forrester's Playmate*, a magazine for young people, published two scripts in play form in 1858. "Dialogue – The Present" in the July 1858 issue dramatized a family discussion about whether one sister in the family should be able to choose how to spend her carefully saved money.[27] The September 1858 issue offered a longer and more elaborate play entitled "Honesty Is the Best Policy."[28] Another children's magazine, *Youth's Casket and Playmate*, published a similar dialogue the following year with the title "Honesty without Policy."[29]

The stories and dramatizations in these magazines for young people were often lessons in morality. "The Dispute," for example, dramatized the naturally changing colors of a chameleon to teach that one should not be tempted to abuse someone who differs from oneself.[30] Occasionally, the purpose for these amusements was simply entertainment, as in a comic tale of a lost love, "And Who Will Guess?"[31]

One of the most popular and long-lasting children's magazines was *St. Nicholas*, first published in 1873. Drama was not a frequent feature, but at least thirteen plays were published in this magazine between 1879 and 193. Some were called comedies, such as the rhymed "Dicky Dot and Dotty Dick," in which the main characters discussed what they would be when they grew up, until being interrupted by a bumble bee,[32] and a one-act comedy entitled "Mrs. Tubb's Telegram."[33]

Parlor dramas for any age did not have a holiday focus until the 1870s and 1880s. The December 1874 issue of *Youth's Companion* offered "new Christmas diversions" to be read or sung. The article "Readings and Ballads with Tableaux" suggested that a vocalist sing ballads that were more "merry" than usual, possibly accompanied by instruments. The musicians and singer stood behind the curtain while actors portrayed scenes suggested by the verse. Possible ballads included Longfellow's "Blind Girl of Castel Guille" and one by James Russel Lowell about Zekel and Hulda entitled "Courtship."[34]

The following December this same periodical offered "Christmas Tableaux" based on the "well known" wax works by Mrs. Jarley. The article stated, "Perhaps no holiday amusement is more deservedly popular with social parties at the present time, than tableaux. They are at once simple and refined, and may be made sufficiently humorous to adapt them admirably to the spirit of the mid-winter festival."[35]

Two Christmas plays for children appeared in *St. Nicholas* in 1889,[36] and another one appeared in *Harper's Young People* at about the same time.[37] *St. Nicholas* waited until 1931, however, to publish another Christmas drama, this time in the form of a marionette show with a six-page script and directions for making the stringed puppets.[38] A play for Valentine's Day appeared in *Harper's Round Table* in February of 1896.[39] Plays for children that included music appeared in 1894[40] and 1903.[41] The *Delineator*, a magazine for women, published two articles in the 1890s suggesting that parlor theatricals be used to celebrate Valentine's Day. The party described in February 1893 used shadow pantomines, in which scenes were created by casting shadows on a wall, and the February 1895 celebration used "masquerades" or charades for its theme.[42] These dramatizations for amateurs were not necessarily intended to be performed only in the home, but many of the early ones were written for small casts, making them suitable for performance in the parlor. As the nineteenth century closed, theatricals as presented in American periodicals changed from impromptu evening entertainments to more elaborate presentations that seemed to require much more preparation. The intent also changed over the years from adult amusements and educational lessons for children to amusement and holiday commemorations for all ages. By 1915, some of the dramatizations were definitely not meant for home production but for more public occasions or for school. The February 1915 issue of *St. Nicholas* offered "Everychild – A School Morality"[43] And a May Day pageant for boys and girls with the title "The Crowning of the Queen" appeared in the May issue.[44]

With a few exceptions, parlor theatricals published in periodicals did not offer much instruction for their presentation. They seemed to rely on the reader's prior knowledge. More about how to produce them was available from instruction books. For example, *The Amateur's Guide to Home Theatricals* gave very complete instructions on how to organize and act in such productions. Detailed instructions for turning the parlor into a theater included directions for drop-scenes, set pieces, stage effects, costumes, make-up, and painting the scenery, even describing how to "mix together whitening and size to a tolerable good consistence" for a primer coat on the scenery cloth.[45]

Scripts for plays were also available from such firms as Peck and Synder; in 1886, its trade catalog offered six pages of play titles for sale at fifteen cents apiece.[46] The modern reader can also obtain a better understanding of this period through recent publications. *Confidence Men and Painted Women* by Karen Halttunen provides information about fashion, etiquette, sentimental ritual, and other cultural threads in America between 1830 and 1870.[47] The role that music played in home entertainment is treated in depth by Nicholas Tawa's *Sweet Songs for Gentle Americans*.[48]

And finally, one should not neglect the personal view of this period of history to be found in diaries and reminiscences. They lend a sense of reality to these forms of amusements that are unfamiliar to us today. Writing in the 1850s in Canadaigua, New York, sixteen-year-old Caroline Cowles Richards left his satisfying description of the enjoyment that these entertainments provided: "February 24, 1858. – The boarders at the Seminary had some tableaux last evening . . . they were splendid. Mr. Chubbuck was in nearly all of them. The most beautiful one was Abraham offering up Isaac. Mr. Chubbuck was Abraham and Sarah Ripley was Isaac. After the tableaux they acted a charade. The word was "Masterpiece." It was fine."[49]

NOTES

[1]Katherine C. Grier, *Culture and Comfort: People, Parlors, and Upholstery, 1850–1930* (Rochester, NY: The Strong Museum, 1988), 59.

[2]Grier, *Culture and Comfort*, 251.

[3]Catherine E. Beecher, *A Treatise on Domestic Economy. For the Use of Young Ladies at Home and at School* (New York: Harper and Brothers, 1858), 244. Beecher's first name was misspelled on the title page of this volume.

[4]Beecher, *Treatise on Domestic Economy*, 245.

[5]Frank Luther Mott, *A History of American Magazines, 1850–1865* (Cambridge, MA: Harvard University Press, 1938), 56.

[6]Mott, *History of American Magazines, 1741–1850*, 581.

[7]Mott, *History of American Magazines, 1850–1865*, 309.

[8]Mott *History of American Magazines, 1741–1850*, 167.

[9]"Charades in Action," *Godey's Lady's Book and Magazine*, December 1854. 515 (hereafter cited as *Godey's*).

[10]"Charades in Action," 515.

[11]Ibid.

[12]Ibid., 516.

[13]Ibid.

[14]"Letter I. – Tableaux Vivants," in "Ella Moore's Letters from the City," *Godey's*, June 1860, 564. Between June and November 1860, *Godey's* published four letters entitled "Ella Moore's Letters from the City." The first and fourth letters were continued over two months.

[15]"Ella Moore's Letters," June 1860, 564–565.

[16]"Ella Moore's Letters," July 1860, 88–89.

[17]"Letter II. – Impromptu Charades," in "Ella Moore's Letters," August 1860, 184–5.

[18]"Letter III. – Proverbs," in "Ella Moore's Letters," September 1860, 282–3.

[19]"Letter IV. – Moving Tableaux," in "Ella Moore's Letters," November 1860, 472.

[20]M. S. S., "Acting Charade. Frenchman," *Godey's*, January 1870, 72–75; S. Annie Frost, "Acting Charade. Checkmate," *Godey's*, May 1870, 446–50.

[21]M. Z. Young, "Charade. – Window-Pane," *Godey's*, February 1873, 192.

[22]Fannie Fancher, "Acting Charade. "There Are None So Blind as Those Who Will Not See," *Godey's*, October 1873, 383–84.

[23]V. Sheffey Haller, "Dining Room," *Godey's*, February 1885, 214–21, and March 1885, 337–43.

24S. Annie Frost, "Man-Age: An Acting Charade," *Peterson's Magazine*, January 1860, 87–89.

25S. Annie Frost, "Antidote: Acting Charade," *Peterson's*, March 1862, 261–63.

26"Dressed for the Charade," frontispiece in *Godey's*, February 1885.

27"Dialogue – The Present," *Forrester's Playmate*," July 1858, 7–9.

28"Honesty Is the Best Policy," *Forrester's Playmate*, September 1858, 75–81.

29"Honesty without Policy," *Youth's Casket and Playmate*, January 1859, 14–17.

30"The Dispute," *Youth's Casket and Playmate*, July 1859, 21–22.

31"And Who Will Guess?," *Youth's Casket and Playmate*, May 1859, 193–97.

32E. S. Brooks, "Comedies for Children. Dicky Dot and Dotty Dick," *St. Nicholas*, February 1886, 285–87.

33Katharine McDowell Rice, "Mrs. Tubb's Telegram," *St. Nicholas*, February 1905, 344.

34"Readings and Ballads with Tableaux," *Youth's Companion*, 24 December 1874, 430.

35"Christmas Tableaux," *Youth's Companion*, 28 December 1875, 423–24.

36Charles A. Murdock, "A Sixteenth Century Christmas," *St. Nicholas*, December 1888, 145; Eudora S. Bumstead, "Waiting for Santa Claus," *St. Nicholas*, January 1889, 222.

37Margaret Sutton Briscoe, "Papa's Rod," *Harper's Young People* 25 December 1894, 140–43.

38Frances Lester Warner, "The Holly Goblin's Christmas Eve," *St. Nicholas*, December 1931, 80–83, 114–15.

39Caroline Creevy, "The Changed Valentine," *Harper's Round Table*, 11 February 1896, 360–63.

40Palmer Cox, "The Brownies in Fairy Land," *St. Nicholas*, March 1894, 462, and April 1894, 535.

41Caroline C. Lovell, "Prince Charming's Fate," *St. Nicholas*, February 1903, 350.

42H. C. W., "A Valentine Shadow Party," *The Delineator*, February 1893, 178–79; H. C. Wood, "A Valentine Masquerade," *The Delineator*, February 1895, 268–69.

43"Everychild – A School Morality," *St. Nicholas*, February 1915, 358–59.

44Jesse M. Baker, "The Crowning of the Queen," *St. Nicholas*, May 1915, 634.

45*The Amateur's Guide to Home Theatricals* (New York: Samuel French, 1866), 19.

46Peck and Synder, *Price List of Out and Indoor Sports and Pastime* (1886; reprint, New York, 1971).

47Karen Halttunen, *Confidence Men and Painted Women: A Study of Middle-class Culture in America, 1830–1870* (New Haven and London: Yale University Press, 1982).

48Nicholas E. Tawa, *Sweet Songs for Gentle Americans: The Parlor Song in America, 1790–1860* (Bowling Green, OH: Bowling Green University Press, 1980).

49Caroline Cowles Richards Clarke, *Diary of Caroline Cowles Richards, 1852–1872* (Canandaigua, NY: 1908), 86.

This article utilizes the research for the workshops and the exhibits and the resources of the Strong Museum library. It uses articles and scripts from nineteenth- and early twentieth-century periodicals to describe dramatic entertainment available for performance in American homes during this period. Adverse attitudes toward theater in general did not relax until the 1850s, at least for the publishers and readers of American periodicals. By the 1860s and 1870s, there seems to have been not only acceptance but an assumption that the readers of these articles were so familiar with the charades, tableaux, and other forms of dramatic entertainment that the scripts could be published without much explanation. By the 1930s, the few scripts that still appeared in the periodicals examined for this study were usually not for home performance but more for public audiences at schools and outdoor pageants.

Sources of information for this article were limited to the periodicals in the Strong Museum Library. I have also listed other libraries in New York State that hold extensive or complete runs.

Delineator. Published in New York and London by the Butterick Publishing Company in the 1890s. Available at the Rochester Museum and Science Center Library and the New York State Historical Association Library in Cooperstown.

Godey's Lady's Book and Magazine. First published in Philadelphia in 1830 as the *Lady's Book*, it contains stories, poems, essays, health and fashion advice, and illustrations, as well as the occasional domestic drama discussed here. In 1892, the magazine moved to New York and merged with *Argosy* at the end of that decade. Available at the Buffalo and Erie County Public Library in Buffalo, Vassar College Library in Poughkeepsie, David A. Howe Public Library in Wellesville, and Queens Borough Public Library in Jamaica.

Harper's Round Table. A magazine for children published in New York City from 1895 to at least 1899. Available at the Queens Borough Public Library in Jamaica, St. Johns University Library in Jamaica, and Jervis Public Library in Rome.

Harper's Young People. Another magazine for children published in New York from November 1879 to April 1895. Available at the University of Rochester Library, the Rochester Public Library, and Hamilton College Library in Clinton.

Peterson's Magazine. Founded in 1842 in Philadelphia, this periodical concentrated on fashions and light literature. A theatrical department was added in 1896, but changes of editorship and ownership ended the magazine's career in 1898, when it was merged into *Argosy*. Available at the University of Rochester Library, Utica College Library, Rochester Museum and Science Center Library, Rochester Public Library, Queens Borough Public Library in Jamaica, and Jervis Public Library in Rome.

St. Nicholas. A popular magazine for children, it was first issued in November 1873 under the editorship of Mary Mapes Dodge. It was published in New York and ran until June 1943. Available at SUNY at Binghamton, SUNY at Buffalo, Mohawk Valley Library Association in Schenectady, Flower Memorial Library in Watertown, Vassar College Library in Poughkeepsie, Finger Lakes Library in Ithaca, and Rochester Public Library.

Youth's Companion. This magazine for young people was published in Boston from 1827 to 1834 and 1836 to 1929. Available at the University of Rochester Library, Flower Memorial Library in Watertown, Rochester Museum and Science Center Library, Onondaga County Public Library in Syracuse, and Jervis Public Library in Rome.

Youth's Casket. This magazine for children was published in Buffalo from 1852–1857. Available at the University of Rochester Library and the New York State Historical Association in Cooperstown.

Youth's Casket and Playmate. A magazine for children published in Boston from at least January 1859 to at least March 1860. Available at Margaret Woodbury Strong Museum Library in Rochester.

[Editor's note: a Preliminary Checklist of Early Printed Children's Plays in English, 1780–1865, by Jonathan Levy and Martha Mahard, appears in *Performing Arts Resources*, Volume XII (1987)].

THE THEATRE AS SEEN
THROUGH LATE NINETEENTH CENTURY
TECHNICAL PERIODICALS

by Jack W. McCullough

The nineteenth century was a period of many changes in theatre architecture and stage machinery. It was an age of inventions, some of which had drastic repercussions in the theatre. Early in the century candles and oil lamps gave way to the more efficient gas lighting systems. At last there was relatively bright illumination and some opportunity for lighting control. But the new invention brought increased hazards with it, for the brilliant jet of gas burned as well as brightened. A rash of theatre fires occurred, many of them truly disastrous, and attention was focussed on how to make theatres safer.[1] Engineers, architects, builders and technicians of all kinds attacked the problem. In the process they not only developed safer construction and better mechanical equipment, they also provided the stage designer with newer and more sophisticated ways to awe and amaze theatre audiences.

The technical specialists, often with international reputations, wrote profusely about their work. They evaluated theatres then in existence, theorized about applications of new technology in the theatre, proposed their plans with elaborate explanations and detailed drawings, and debated at length about the values of

JACK W. MCCULLOUGH is an Associate Professor of Communication and Theatre at Trenton State College in New Jersey. He is an author of *Living Pictures on the New York Stage* (Ann Arbor: UMI Research Press, 1983) and has published articles in the *Journal of Popular Culture*, *The Polish Review*, and *Theatre Survey*. He is currently working on a study of living pictures on the twentieth century stage.

their ideas. All of this may be found in the late nineteenth century issues of non-theatre technical journals—publications in such fields as architecture, engineering, mechanics, and even sanitation.

Many arts and sciences find expression in the theatre, but it is surprising to find that theatre research is frequently rather introspective, written to the theatre about the theatre, without adequate consideration of resources in those fields which exist apart from the theatre. References to non-theatre, technical publications are rare in theatre journals, textbooks, histories, and other theatre literature, both during the nineteenth century and afterward.

This brief study will attempt to provide a taste of the vast quantity of theatre resource material available in a few science and technology periodicals and to suggest some directions in which further study might profitably proceed. This study does not hope to exhaust the material in any type of publication, nor does it completely survey the work published in any period. It is meant to sample available resources and perhaps promote more thorough use of such materials in future studies.

The study begins with some comments about the periodicals themselves, followed by a descriptive evaluation of some of the materials they contain. Finally, an extended example, in the form of one major series of articles, will be described in some detail. Appendices and bibliography provide lists of both the source materials and the periodicals.

I. The Publications[2]

Technical publications in the late nineteenth century ranged from those with a popular orientation through what might be called "trade magazines" to scholarly journals of professional societies, government agencies, and academic institutions. *Work*, which began publication in 1889, carried the subtitle, "An Illustrated Magazine of Practice and Theory for All Workmen, Professional and Amateur." *Architecture and Building* called itself "A Magazine Devoted to Contemporary Architectural Construction," and *Electrical Engineer* was subtitled "A Weekly Review of Theoretical and Applied Electricity."

Many technical and professional organizations and societies existed in the United States during the 1800's. All of the organizations in the list of examples below published some form of regular periodical. The date given indicates the year publication began, but, of course, the organization often existed long before it began publication.

Some Technical Organizations

American Institute of Electrical Engineers	1884
American Society of Civil Engineers	1852
Architectural League of New York	1881
Arkansas Society of Engineers, Architects,	
and Surveyors	1887
Association of Engineering Societies	1881
Boston Society of Civil Engineers	1879
Electric Club of New York	1886(87?)
Engineers' and Architects' Association of	
Southern California	1895
Master Builders' Exchange	1886
Mechanics' Institute	1833
National Electric Light Association	1885
National Association of American Inventors	1878
Western Association of Architects	1883

These organizations are only a few of the many active technical societies in America before 1900. It should be noted, too, that they were not limited to the eastern theatre centers, and they include a wide spectrum of technological areas.

The profusion of publications sometimes presents difficulties in tracking down references. Frequently, more than one journal used the same title. The title, *Architectural Era*, for instance, referred to two publications simultaneously during 1887-1893.[3] *Architectural Review* was published in Boston, 1891-1910, but an earlier publication in Philadelphia, 1868-1870, was called *The Architectural Review and American Builders' Journal. Builder* was published in Pittsburgh, 1886-1919, but a London magazine of the same name began in 1842 and is still published. Two *Electrical Engineer* journals were published in London and New York during the same year, 1884, although they were entirely separate publications. *Engineer* in New York overlapped *The Engineer* in London from 1887 until the New York magazine merged into *power* in 1908.

As is true in all fields, there are many periodicals whose titles do not clearly indicate their content. *Brochure Series* contains architectural illustrations. *Compass*, a magazine of more general content, contains material "for Engineers, Surveyors, Architects, Draughtsmen, and Students." *Progressive Age* began as *Water Gas Journal* and later added an interest in electricity.

Iron Age stands as a rare example of those few publications which adopted a simple name and retained it unchanged. Today's

Iron Age has been *Iron Age* since its beginning in 1859. Titles of most publications, on the other hand, have changed at least slightly from time to time; some have seen bewildering alterations. *Manufacturers' Chronicle* began as *Brick, Tile and Metal Review*, and *The World's Progress* became *American Inventor* for its last ten years.

Research problems are compounded by the lack of adequate indexes. *Poole's Index to Periodical Literature*, which covers the period, 1802-1906, virtually ignores technical journals. *A Contents-Subject Index to General and Periodical Literature* (London, 1900) by Alfred Cotgreave includes a few entries of articles describing theatres and scenic practices, but none from technical publications.

A few references to early periodical articles may be found in some more recent indexes and bibliographies, but even these are severely limited in scope.[4] Perhaps the best bibliography of technical literature related to theatre in the nineteenth century was published 27 July 1896 in the *American Architect and Building News* (v. 52, pp. 125-127) and was compiled by William Paul Gerhard, a frequent contributor to the architectural journals. The contents of Gerhart's bibliography is listed in Appendix B.

Many individual publications provide index supplements for each volume. Those for *Scientific American, Scientific American Supplement*, and *The Building News and Engineering Journal* are extremely useful, but even a cursory look through the pages of most other journal indexes reveals that articles are either not listed at all or are listed under subject heading with no mention of "theatre," "stage," "scenery," or any similar term meaningful to the theatre scholar.

In short, while there is a wealth of theatre information hidden in these periodicals, there is no convenient, systematic way of discovering it at present.

II. Evaluation of Materials

Material in the technical journals ranges in length from brief paragraphs in such "chatty" columns as "Notes and Clippings" in *American Architect and Building News* to long serialized articles extending over several years of publication.[5]

Several characteristics of these articles are notable. First, the style, while not always exciting, is usually precise and clear. If the article is meant to instruct, the author painstakingly develops the smallest detail. If the approach is argumentative, a strong case is built, which relies on clear explanation and logical construction rather than emotional appeal. The authors seem to enjoy the theatrical effects they describe, but their real satisfaction seems to come from their cool, exact explanation of how those effects are achieved. The following description from an unsigned news article in 1896 may illustrate:

> In the midst of a desperate battle a shell falls and bursts upon the stage. . . . A papier mache shell formed of separate pieces glued together contains the quantity of powder strictly sufficient to separate the pieces and produce the bursting. In the powder there is an electric primer which is ignited by a current of three amperes and which is connected by wires, on the one hand, with an interrupter and, on the other, with the main conductor of the lighting circuit of the theatre. At one of the sides of the stage, out of sight of the spectators, there is a small cannon whose charge is ignited in the same way and by means of the same interrupter. At the proper moment a man throws the shell. The latter bursts, and the spectators, hearing the loud explosion of the cannon at the same instant, imagine that the harmless cardboard envelope is the cause of the formidable detonation.[6]

Additional clarity is usually provided by illustrations in the forms of photographs, engravings, or excellent line drawings. Drawings are usually engineers' or architects' drawings presented in sizes adequate to permit considerable detail. Also, the photogravure process and paper quality used generally resulted in high quality reproduction of the illustrations.

A second notable characteristic of these sources is that they reveal an intentional "cross-fertilization" of ideas among designers and technicians of many countries. *Scientific American Supplement* carried detailed reports of the new revolving stage at the Court Theatre in Munich in 1896 and of its inventor, Carl Lautenschlaeger, mechanical director of the Royal Theatre of Bavaria.[7] *Scientific American* provided a full description of new lighting equipment and control systems at Covent Garden in 1899.[8] A British publication, *The Building News and Engineering Journal*, devoted an article to "Theatre Regulations in New York" (5 August 1892, 195-196), and, in another issue, carried the full text of John C. Hexamer's paper, "The Construction and Interior Arrangement of Theatres," which was originally presented at a meeting of the Franklin Institute in Philadelphia.[9] A series of seven articles in *American Architect and Building News* was devoted to comparisons of theatre building regulations in England, America, and countries of continental Europe and

Asia.[10] "Theatrical Stage Arrangements and Machinery," by Alphonse Warington, compares English and German theatres and recommends that English architects examine plans of the Victoria Theatre in Berlin as a model of excellence.[11]

This "cross-fertilization" was further promoted by the frequent publication of scholarly and professional papers and reports. John C. Hexamer's paper at the Franklin Institute has already been mentioned; there were many others. William Paul Gerhard, Consulting Engineer for Sanitary Works in New York City, presented a fifty-page paper, "Water Service and Fire Protection," at the thirteenth annual convention of the New England Water Works Association. The paper was published in the Association's *Journal* and condensed in *Engineering News*.[12] *The Building News* carried not only the scholarly papers presented before the London Architectural Association, but also a transcript of questions and discussion of the papers.[13] In 1882 the *American Architect and Building News*, in a two-part series, printed the text of a report entitled "The Construction and Arrangement of Theatres," unanimously approved by the Austrian Society of Engineers and Architects.[14]

A third characteristic of these materials is the range of theatre subject matter treated. A suggestion of this range is already apparent from the examples previously cited, however some analysis of those areas most strongly emphasized may be helpful.

The most numerous articles are those which deal with the design and construction of theatres themselves. These theories and practices are presented in great detail as a comprehensive treatment of the subject. Most notable in this group are the Emden paper cited above (See note 13.), a series of thirty-one articles by Edwin O. Sachs,[15] and an even longer series of forty-seven articles by Ernest A. E. Woodrow.[16] These and other writers were concerned with all aspects of theatre building. They discussed design in terms of an artistically pleasing architectural structure; a workable plant for manager, scene technician, and actor; a comfortable and convenient accommodation for the audience; and a building which ensured the safety of all who used it. For reasons suggested earlier, this last concern often assumed primary importance. The general articles extensively treat questions of safety, especially protection from fire. Many articles dealt exclusively with this subject.[17]

A second approach these writers took was to describe and evaluate the construction of theatres already in existence. *The Building News* (6 January 1882,) gave a description of Wallack's Theatre under the headline, "An Improved Theatre." *Engineering*

Record (11 August 1900) described "The Folly Theatre, Brooklyn" because it was the first New York theatre to be erected under new building codes which had gone into effect 23 December 1899. Another lengthy series of articles by Woodrow devotes each of twenty-three installments to detailed descriptions of separate theatres.[18]

Many articles dealt with specific kinds of stage machinery and equipment, often in relation to a particular theatre. These descriptions usually announced new applications of technology to theatre. Steele Mackaye's famous elevator stage at the Madison Square Theatre was reported and illustrated in duplicate articles in both *Scientific American* and its *Supplement*.[19] Another version of the same account was carried in London by *The Engineer*.[20] The London article added this interesting bit of incidental intelligence:

> Not a little fun . . . was made of Mr. Steele Mackaye in 1879, when he obtained his patent for and proposed to build the first movable stage. . . . The details of Mr. Mackaye's patent were not as completely worked out, although the idea was there, as they subsequently were by Mr. Nelson Waldron, the stage machinist, who elaborated the system and obtained a subsequent patent therefor, under which these movable stages have been so successfully and satisfactorily operated at the Madison Square Theatre.[21]

Considerable attention was paid to the application of hydraulic power to operation of stage machinery. Walter Emden mentions the possibility in a discussion of a proposal for distribution of hydraulic power in London.[22] In a letter to the editor of *Engineering* (1 October 1897, 419–420), Edwin O. Sachs defends the use of hydraulic machinery at Drury Lane Theatre; an accident had occurred there, possibly caused by faulty hydraulic equipment.

Increased use of electricity resulted in numerous reports of theatre applications for lighting and for motorized equipment. *Scientific American Supplement* described the complex motor-driven scenic effects at the Union Square Theatre, used to provide the spectacular live horse race in Neil Burgess' play, *The County Fair*.[23] The accompanying illustration, a cut-away view of the stage, reveals the liberal use of electric motors to control treadmills for the galloping horses, a moving "panorama-roll" backdrop, a moving picket fence at the edge of the racetrack, and fans to blow the jockeys' silks. In an article romantically entitled "The

Temple of Electricity," M. J. Sullivan enthusiastically described the extent to which electric lights were used in Madison Square Garden.[24]

A third kind of subject matter was the treatment of stagecraft and related techniques. In the publication, *Work*, William Corbould presented several groups of articles during 1891–1899. The first explained how to execute perspective drawings for stage design;[25] the second treated stage carpentry techniques.[26] The tone of the articles resembles that of a modern handbook for community theatre technicians. Occasionally information from more general sources found its way into the technical publications. In 1881 *Scientific American Supplement* (v. 12, p. 4622) reprinted "art on the Stage," an essay about scene painting, which had appeared originally in the *New York Tribune*. In addition to describing a step-by-step procedure for painting scenery, it also listed prices of color pigments and other materials and described the use of metallic papers, "glitter," and other specialties.

Special scenic effects for particular plays are the subject of many articles. Several examples of these have already been presented.

Finally, there is a body of material which defies classification. *The American Contractor*, for instance, contains no articles of the sort discussed so far. Its masthead states, "The object of this Publication is to furnish Advance Reports of Building Projects, before the closing of contracts, for the special use of Material Men, Supply Men, Manufacturers, Contractors, Builders, Architects, Decorators, . . . etc."[27] A typical entry reads: "South Bend, Ind. – D. M. Shively is considering the matter of remodeling his large brick block into an opera house."[28] Interestingly, *The American Contractor* carries "Theatres" as a regular classification in its table of contents.

Other miscellany includes such varied items as "Notes upon the Architectural Works of Charles Garnier," designer of the Paris Opera House,[29] or this filler paragraph entitled "Theatres and Population:"

There is a theatre in Paris for every 32,000 inhabitants, one in Berlin for 81,000, one in Bordeaux for 84,000, one in Budapest for 85,000, one in Hamburg for 113,000, one in Vienna for 138,000, and one in London for 145,000. There are more theatres, proportionately to the population, in Italy than in any other country, there being one to 9,800 inhabitants in Cantania, one to 15,000 in Florence, one to 20,000 in Bologna, one to

24,000 at Venice, one to 30,000 at Milan and Turin, and one to 31,000 in Rome.[30]

Sometimes the reader derives far more than sheer information. Read between the lines of this brief item, for instance:

> Science plays a more or less prominent part in the theatrical business of today. The Parisian papers, both secular and scientific, have been devoting columns to the appearance in Paris of some American vaudevillists of the gentler sex whose dresses were bedecked with hundreds of minute incandescent lamps.[31]

Finally, consider the reaction of a theatre manager who, in 1895, might have read the following account of a new theatre heating system which employed – believe it or not – electric radiators.

> The average temperature of the theatre inside after the radiators have been working a reasonable time is about 60 degrees when the corridors are about 40 degrees. Arrangements have now been made for warming the stage, and, no doubt, this will prevent the passage of the cold currents of air usually experienced when the curtain is raised. The current taken by each large portable radiator is 12 amperes, and the small box radiators take 3 amperes each, making, in all, a total of 114 amperes, but, as only 2 of the large radiators are found necessary, the current actually used for warming the auditorium is 90 amperes at 100 volts. Thus it can be seen that 9 kilowatts per hour are required when the whole apparatus is in full work, and the cost, at 8 cents per unit, is 72 cents per hour. To warm the theatre, therefore, for a period of 4 hours the cost is $2.88.[32]

III. An Extended Example: Edwin O. Sachs, "Modern Theatre Stages," *Engineering*, v. 61-63, 17 January 1896-11 June 1897.

This enormous study of theatre stages of differing kinds is one of the most extensive and useful works contained in nineteenth century technical journals. It combines the approach of investigating design and construction theory with that of describing and evaluating contemporary theatre buildings. Much of the content of this series was subsequently re-edited and published as "Stage Construction," a supplement to Sachs' three-volume work, *Modern Opera Houses and Theatres*, produced in collaboration with Ernest A. E. Woodrow,[33] Woodrow collaborated on the first volume only, but much of his contribution to the book, may be found also in his own long series of articles on theatre construction.[34] The following summary of the Sachs series in intended to reveal, by extended example, some of the characteristics described in the preceding parts of this paper. While the series is long, it is not the longest; it treated the same kinds of contents other authors chose; its methods, style, and attitudes are rather typical of technical writing of the period.

Numbers 1-3. "Introduction" (17 January 1896, 71; 31 January 1896, 139-142; 14 February 1896, 205-207).

Sachs sets forth his purpose in these words: "I now propose to show to what extent modern sciences and methods have already been brought into the service of stage management. . . . I do not intend to formulate any 'model' requirements. . . . The series will be limited to the explanation of typical examples of stages erected during the last 25 years, and in full working order at the present time." (p. 72) Illustrations in this first section include drawings of the floor plan, gridiron, and the third tier of flies at the Paris National Opera House. Part of Number 3 is devoted to a discussion and illustration of a contracting proscenium opening designed by a Professor Herkamer.

Numbers 4-5. "The English Wooden Stage" (28 February 1896, 271-276; 13 March 1896, 333-335)

This section describes "the stage of an ordinary provincial or suburban theatre of today." (p. 271) Architectural characteristics, machinery, rigging, and scenic units are described. Illustrations include floor plans, lateral and longitudinal section drawings of the stage house, details of bridges and sliders, and various pieces of scenic equipment.

Numbers 6-7. "The French Wooden Stage" (10 April 1896, 459-463; 24 April 1896, 538-539)

The Eden Theatre, Paris, and the Flemish Theatre, Brussels, are used as examples of what Sachs considers to be rather old-fashioned construction. Illustrations are large and clear, showing many details of scenic machinery.

Number 8. "The German Wooden Stage" (8 May 1896, 593-597)

Special attention in this section is placed on descriptions of traps and cuts, which differentiate the German stage from that of other countries. A brief introductory explanation of gas lighting is provided. Two pages of large illustrations include drawings of the Vienna Court Opera House and the Dresden Court Theatre.

Numbers 9-15. "Wood and Iron Stages" (22 May 1896, 663-667; 12 June 1896, 768-772; 3 July 1896, 3-7; 17 July 1896, 66-68, 70-71; 31 July 1896, 133-135; 14 August 1896, 193-196; 21 August 1896, 230-232).

Theatres used as examples of this somewhat better type of construction include the Paris National Opera House, the Rotterdam Theatre, D'Oyly Carte's English Opera House, the Reims and Schwerin Theatres, and several smaller theatres. The Reims Theatre is singled out as a "typical modern theatre" by Sachs. This section includes a more complete description of gas lighting for both stage and backstage uses. There are numerous illustrations of items of stage hardware: tie-off cleats, sheaves, devices for joining wood and iron, etc.

Number 16. "Iron Stages. – The Amsterdam Municipal Theatre" (11 September 1896, 325-327; plate following p. 340)

To Sachs, this stage is what a modern theatre should be. He praises its totally iron construction not only from the standpoint of fire safety, but also for its dependability of scenic operation.

Numbers 17-19. "The 'Asphaleia' Stage" (25 September 1896, 387-390; 23 October 1896, 513-517; 13 November 1896, 601-614)

The "Asphaleia" Stage is a type of stage which employed elaborate hydraulic scenic machinery. The name derives from a business syndicate which financed the construction. Sachs considers the two most important "Asphaleia" stages to be those at Halle and Budapest, and these are described and illustrated in detail, with special emphasis on the hydraulic equipment. Number 19 also provides an illustration of such a stage at the Chicago Auditorium.

Numbers 20-22. "The 'Hofburg' Theatre at Vienna" (27 November 1896, 661-665; 18 December 1896, 755-758; 25 December 1896, 793-796)

Sachs points out, "In the 'Hofburg' Theatre we find a stage that has been built regardless of expense, with the intention of being a model of construction in every respect; and, at the same time, we find those in charge, thanks to their command of ample funds, are able to keep the installation in most perfect order." (p. 661) History and design of this theatre is developed through text and drawings.

Numbers 23-24. "Stages by Fritz Brandt at Wiesbaden, Essen, and Berlin" (8 January 1897, 35-39; 29 January 1897, 127-131)

In addition to general description of these theatres, much of this section is devoted to two inventions by Fritz Brandt, Engineer-in-Chief at the Court Playhouses in Berlin. The first invention is a combination of hydraulic and cable driven bridges at the Berlin Court Theatre. The second is a device for moving the orchestra floor in front of the stage. As usual, illustrations provide further clarification.

Numbers 25–26. "The Munich 'Electric' Turntable Stage" (12 February 1897, 201–205, plate following p. 210; 26 February 1897, 267–271)

Although the Munich turntable was explained in several different journals, this is the most complete description with more and clearer illustrations than elsewhere. Of particular interest is a nine-part series of floor plans showing scene shifts for a production of *Don Juan*. Six of these keyed to watercolor sketches of the designer's renderings of the scenes (reproduced here in monochrome).

Numbers 27–30. Safety from Fires; Fire-resisting Curtains" (12 March 1897, 331–333; 26 March 1897, 392–393; 9 April 1897, 461–466; 23 April 1897, 533–534)

This section considers theatre location, construction type, materials, heating, lighting, ventilation, and use of fire-fighting equipment. Various asbestos and metal fire curtain installations are discussed. A digression in Number 29 treats the hydraulic stage machinery at Drury Lane Theatre.

Number 31. "Conclusion" (11 June 1897, 767–768)

This article simply summarizes the content and approach taken throughout the series.

IV. Conclusions

It is evident that theatre material is plentiful in technical journals of the late nineteenth century. The material deals with a wide variety of subjects from architectural design to the means for achieving the most specific stage illusion. It treats the history of theatre design, the business and management of theatres, and the relation of theatre to governmental regulation. It introduces people who, literally, helped shape the physical theatre, and it helps reveal the interdependence among theatres in different parts of the world.

Much of this material, however, is not conveniently available to theatre scholars. Publications, themselves, are often poorly indexed, and indexes prepared from a "theatre point of view" are so rare and incomplete as to provide little or no help.

The happy fact is that publications cited in this study, and other publications like them, are readily available in many libraries and collections. It is hoped that this preliminary sampling will draw attention to these remarkable sources in a new

light and result in more effective use of them as a means to discover the more complete heritage of today's theatre.

NOTES

[1]Edwin O. Sachs, *Fires and Public Entertainments* (London, 1897), provides "a
study of some 1100 notable fires at theatres, music halls, circus buildings,
and temporary structures during the last 100 years."

[2]A complete list of publications mentioned in the text may be found in Appendix A.

[3]Information regarding publication dates and title changes may be found in
the *Union List of Serials in Libraries of the United States and Canada*, 3rd
Ed., 5 vols., E. B. Titus, ed. (New York, 1965). Frank Luther Mott, *A
History of American Magazines* (Cambridge, MA, 1957), treats some spe-
cialized publications, and a few references may be found in William L.
Chenery, "American Magazines 1741-1941," *Bulletin of the New York Public Library*, June 1941, and in F. J. Hoffman, Charles Allen, and Carolyn
Ulrich, *The Little Magazine: A History and a Bibliography* (Princeton,
1946).

[4]The New York Public Library, *The Development of Scenic Art and Stage
Machinery*, a bibliography compiled by William Burt Gamble (New York,
1928); Columbia University Library, Avery Architectural Library, *Avery
Index to Architectural Periodicals* (Boston, 1963); *The Engineering Index*
(New York, 1884-1899); Francis Ellis Galloupe, *Galloupe's General Index
to Engineering Periodicals* (Boston, 1888-1893), which covers the period
1883-1892.

[5]A number of examples presented below will illustrate the variation in length.
One long series of articles is described more fully in Part III.

[6]"Electricity in the Theatre," *Scientific American Supplement*, 10 October
1896, 17332.

[7]"Lautenschlaeger's New Revolving Stage," *Scientific American Supplement*,
29 August 1896, 17230-17231.

[8]"Electric Lighting at the Covent Garden Theatre," *Scientific American*, 30
September 1899, 211.

[9]John C. Hexamer, "The Construction and Interior Arrangement of Theatres,"
The Building News and Engineering Journal, 15 July 1892, 65-67.

[10]Ernest A. E. Woodrow, "Theatre Building Regulations," *American Architect
and Building News*, 16 April-20 August 1892.

[11]*Builder*, 20 April 1861, 261.

[12]*Engineering News and American Railway Journal*, 21 June 1894, 518.

[13]An excellent example is Walter Emden's paper entitled "Theatres." The
paper and discussion about it may be found in *The Building News and
Engineering Journal*, 23 March 1883, 349-352.

[14]25 March 1882, 138-140; 8 April 1882, 162-164.

[15]"Modern Theatre Stages," *Engineering*, 17 January 1896-11 June 1897. A
description of the content of this series appears in Part III of this paper.

[16]"Theatres," *The Building News and Engineering Journal*, 15 July 1892-28
December 1894.

17William Paul Gerhart makes the most extensive use of this approach in his series of four articles, "The Essential Conditions of Safety in Theatres," *American Architect and Building News*, 23 June; 7, 14, 21 July 1894.

18Ernest A. E. Woodrow, "Theatres," *American Architect and Building News*, 14 April 1894–22 February 1896. These articles should not be confused with Woodrow's longer series, under the same title, which treats general design and construction. (See note 16.)

19"Movable Theatre Stages;" *Scientific American*, 5 April 1884, 209–210; *Scientific American Supplement*, 30 August 1884, 7210–7211.

20"Theatrical Machinery," *The Engineer*, 25 April 1884, 311.

21Ibid.

22"Hydraulic Power for Working the Stage," *Proceedings*, Institution of Civil Engineers, London, 24 April 1888, 66. The article is part of a discussion of Paper No. 2314, "The Distribution of Hydraulic Power in London," by E. B. Ellington.

23"Electricity Behind the Stage," *Scientific American Supplement*, 3 May 1890, 11954–11955.

24*Electrical World*, 14 November 1891, 363–364.

25"Stage Perspective," *Work*, 19 September, 3, 24 October 1891.

26"Stage Carpentry," *Work*, 21 November, 19 December 1891; 23 January, 27 February 1892.

271 December 1894, 25.

28*The American Contractor*, 1 December 1894, 32.

29J. R. Coolidge, Jr., *Architectural Review*, September 1898.

30"Notes and Clippings," *American Architect and Building News*, 22 September 1894, 112. The entire item is quoted.

31"Electrical Notes," *Scientific American Supplement*, 8 March 1899, 19413.

32"A Theatre Heated by Electricity," *American Architect and Building News*, 1 June 1895, 92.

33Edwin O. Sachs and Ernest A. E. Woodrow, *Modern Opera Houses and Theatres: Examples Selected from Playhouses Recently Erected in Europe*, 3 vols. (London, 1896–1898). The Supplements in Volume 3 include "Stage Construction," "Theatre Fires," and "Protective Legislation." "Theatre Fires" was also published separately (See note 1.), and "Protective Legislation" seems to include most of the material in Woodrow's series of articles, "Theatre Building Regulations" (See note 10.).

34Op. Cit. (Note 16).

APPENDIX A

Some Technical Publications of the Late Nineteenth Century

(The following publications are listed by the titles that can be found in the *Union List of Serials*. Title changes prior to 1900 are also shown.)

American Builder: A Journal of Industrial Art. New York, 1868-1894.
   Mar 1868-Jun 1873: *American Builder and Journal of Art.*
   Jan 1880-Mar 1893: *Builder and Woodworker.*
   Apr-Dec 1893: *Architectural Era.*
   Jan-1 Nov 1894: *Builder and Woodworker.*
   Merged into *National Builder.*
American Architect and Building News. Boston, New York; 1876-1908.
American Contractor. Chicago, New York; 1879-21 June 1930.
   Superceded by *General Building Contractor.*
American Electrician. New York, Dec 1898-Dec 1905.
   1889-Apr 1896: *Electrical Industries.*
   Merged into *Electrical World.*
American Institute of Electrical Engineers. *Transactions.* 1884+.
American Society of Civil Engineers. *Proceedings.* New York, Nov 1873-Jan 1950.
American Society of Civil Engineers. *Transactions.* New York, 1867+.
Architect, Builder, and Woodworker. Chicago, New York; Mar 1868-May 1895.
   See *American Builder: A Journal of Industrial Art.*
Architects' and Mechanics' Journal. New York, 1859-1861(?).
Architects' Electrical Bulletin. New York, 1892-Jun 1896(?).
Architectural and Building Monthly. New York, 1890-1894.
Architectural Era. New York, 1864-1893.
   Merged into *Builder and Woodworker.*
Architectural Era. Syracuse, Philadelphia; Jan 1887-Mar 1893.
Architectural Forum. Boston, 1892+.
   1892-1916: *Brickbuilder.*
Architectural League of New York. *Proceedings.* New York, 18 Jan 1881-Mar 1889.
Architectural Record. New York, Jul 1891+.
Architectural Review. Boston, 2 Nov 1891-Apr 1910.

Architectural Review and American Builders' Journal. Philadelphia, 1868–1870.

Architectural Reviewer. Chicago, 1897 (3 issues).

Architectural Sketchbook. Boston, 1873–1876.

Architecture and Building: A Magazine Devoted to Contemporary Architectural Construction. New York, Oct 1882–Mar 1932.
   Oct 1882–Dec 1885: *Building: An Architectural Monthly.*
   Jan 1886–Dec 1889: *Building: An Architectural Weekly.*
   Jan 1890–5 Aug 1899: *Architecture and Building.*
   Oct 1899–Feb 1911: *Architects' and Builders' Magazine.*

Arkansas Society of Architects, Engineers, and Surveyors. *Transactions.* Little Rock, 1887–1889.

Association of Engineering Societies. *Journal.* New York, Nov 1881–Dec 1915.

Boston Society of Civil Engineers. *Proceedings.* Boston, Sep 1879–Jun 1881.

Brick. Chicago, 1894–1910.

Brick and Clay Record. Chicago, Jul 1892+.
   Jul 1892–Dec 1910: *Clay Record.*

Brochure Series. Boston, 1889–1892.

Brochure Series of Architectural Illustration. Boston, 1895–1903.

Builder; an illustrated weekly magazine. London, 31 Dec 1842+.
   7 Jan–11 Feb 1843: not issued.

Builder; devoted to architecture. Pittsburgh, 1886–May 1919.
   1886–1904: *Builders' Gazette.*

Builder, Decorator, and Woodworker. Philadelphia, 1883–Dec 1891.
   1883–Nov 1886: *Builder and Real Estate Advocate.*
   Dec 1886–Mar 1889: *Builder and Decorator.*

Building Age. New York, 1879–Sep 1930.

Building Budget. A Journal of Architecture and Kindred Arts. Chicago, Mar 1885–1890.

Building News and Engineering Journal. London, 1854–Mar 1926.
   1854–1864: *Building News.*
   1865–1872: *Building News and Architectural Review.*

Building Trades Magazine. Scranton, PA; Jul 1897–Oct 1899.
   Jul 1897–Dec 1898: *Home Study for the Building Trades.*
   United with others to form *Science and Industry.*

Building Witness. Cincinnati, 1883+.
   1883–Dec 1912: *Western Architect and Builder.*
   2 Jan–6 Feb 1913: *Building News.*

Cassier's Magazine; Engineering Illustrated. New York, Nov 1891–Sep 1913.

Compass; a monthly journal. . . . New York, 1 Aug 1891–Jul 1894.

Electric Club of New York. *Papers Read Before the Club.* New York, Nov 1886(7?)-Sep 1891.
Electrical Age. New York, Atlanta; 1883-Jun 1910.
  1883-May 1886: *Telegrapher's Advocate.*
  Jun 1886-Jan 1891: *Electric Age.*
  Feb 1891-Jun 1903: *Electrical Age.*
  Jul-Dec 1903: *Electrical and Engineering Age.*
  United with *Southern Electrician* to form *Electrical Engineering.*
Electrical Engineer. London, 1882-9 Feb 1912.
  1882-1883: *Electric Light.*
Electrical Engineer. New York, 1882-2 Mar 1899.
  1882-1883: *Electrician.*
  1884-1887: *Electrician and Electrical Engineer.*
  1888-Mar 1890: *Electrical Engineer; a monthly review* . . .
  Merged into *Electrical World.*
Electrical News and Engineering. Toronto, 1891+.
  1891-1901: *Canadian Electrical News.*
Electrical Progress and Development. Boston, 1886-1892.
  1886: *Modern Light.*
  1887-1889: *Modern Light and Heat.*
Electrical Review. London, 15 Nov 1872+.
  15 Nov-15 Dec 1872: *Telegraphic Journal and Illustrated Review of Electrical Science.*
  Jan 1873-25 Dec 1891: *Telegraphic Journal and Electrical Review.*
Electrical Review. New York, 15 Feb 1882+.
  15 Feb-1 Jun 1882: *New York Review of the Telegraph and Telephone.*
  15 Jun 1882-1 Mar 1883: *Review of the Telegraph and Telephone.*
  22 Mar 1883-Oct 1908: *Electrical Review.*
  7 Nov 1908-Mar 1933: various titles.
  After Mar 1933: *Factory.*
Electrical World. New York, 1883+.
  1883: *Operator and Electrical World.*
  11 Mar-24 Jun 1899: *Electrical World and Electrical Engineer.*
  1 Jul 1899-Dec 1905: *Electrical World and Engineer.*
Electricity, A Popular Electrical Journal. New York, 22 Jul 1891-4 Apr 1906.
Engineer. With Which is Incorporated Steam Engineering. New York, Cleveland, Chicago; 1881-1 Apr 1908.
  1881-1887: *Mechanical Engineer.*
  Merged into *Power.*

Engineer. London, 1856+.

Engineering: An Illustrated Weekly Journal. London, 5 Jan 1866+.

Engineering Mechanics. Philadelphia, New York; 1882-Nov 1899.

1882-1891: *Mechanics.*

Engineering News-Record. Chicago, Apr 1874+.

Apr 1874: *Engineer and Surveyor.*

May-Dec 1874: *Engineer, Architect, and Surveyor.*

Jan 1875-May 1882: *Engineering News.*

May 1882-Feb 1888: *Engineering News and American Contract Journal.*

Feb 1888-21 Aug 1902: *Engineering News and American Railway Journal.*

28 Aug 1902-29 Mar 1917: *Engineering News; a Journal of Civil Engineering and Construction.*

The Engineering Record, Building Record, and Sanitary Engineer. New York, Dec 1877-Mar 1917.

1877-Nov 1880: *Plumber and Sanitary Engineer.*

Dec 1880-Oct 1886: *Sanitary Engineer.*

Nov 1886-1 Oct 1887: *Sanitary Engineer and Construction Record.*

8 Oct 1887-Nov 1890: *Engineering and Building Record and the Sanitary Engineer.*

Engineers' and Architects' Association of Southern California. *Proceedings.* Los Angeles, 1895-1907.

Home and Country. New York, Jan 1893-May 1897.

Jan 1893-Jan 1895: *Quarterly Illustrator.*

Oct 1895-Jan 1897: *Monthly Illustrator and Home and Country.*

Inland Architect and News Record. Chicago, Feb 1883-Dec 1908.

Iron Age. Middletown, NY; New York; Apr 1859+.

1 Apr 1868-Dec 1872: never published(?).

Monthly to 1863; weekly after.

Journal of Electricity, Power, and Gas. San Francisco, Jul 1895+.

Jul-Aug 1895: *Electrical Journal.*

Sep 1895-Jun 1899: *Journal of Electricity.*

Kansas City Architect and Builder. Kansas City, MO; 1886-Mar 1907.

Manufacturers' Chronicle. Pittsburgh, Mar 1881-Jun 1890.

1881-Sep 1887: *Brick, Tile, and Metal Review.*

Master Builders' Exchange. (See *Kansas City Architect and Builder*)

Mechanics' Magazine and Journal of the Mechanics' Institute. New York, 1833-15 Aug 1837.

Merged into *American Railway Journal.*

Modern Architectural Design and Details. New York, 1881-Mar 1890.

National Builder. Chicago, 1885–Oct 1924.
  1885–Sep 1897: *Hill's National Builder.*
National Electric Light Association. *Proceedings.* New York, 1885–1932.
New York Sketchbook of Architecture. New York, 1874–Dec 1876.
Power. New York, 1880+.
  1880–1884: *Steam.*
  1885–1891: *Power-Steam.*
Power Engineering. Philadelphia, Chicago; 1896+.
  1896–15 Aug 1917: *Practical Engineering.*
  Sep 1917–Dec 1947: *Power Plant Engineering.*
  Jan 1948–Apr 1950: *Power Generation.*
Practical Electricity. Boston, Aug 1887–Mar 1893.
Practical Engineer. Philadelphia, 1897–Dec 1908.
Progressive Age. New York, 1883+.
  1883: *Water Gas Journal.*
  1884–1889: *Progressive Age and Water Gas Journal.*
  1890–1912: *Progressive Age; Gas – Electricity – Water.*
Royal Society of Arts. *Journal.* London, 26 Nov 1852+.
Scientific American. New York, 25 Aug 1845+.
Scientific American Building Monthly. New York, Nov 1885–Jun 1905.
  1885–Dec 1894: *Scientific American Architects' and Builders' Edition.*
  1895–1901: *Scientific American Building Edition.*
Scientific American Supplement. New York, 1876–1919.
Scientific Artisan. Cincinnati, 19 Aug 1858–30 Jun 1860.
Sibley Journal of Engineering. Ithaca, NY (Cornell University, Sibley College), 1887–Jun 1935.
  1887–1891: *Crank.*
  1891–1892: *Crank, Sibley Journal of Engineering.*
Western Association of Architects. (See *Inland Architect and News Record.*)
Western Electrician. Chicago, 1887–31 Oct 1908.
Work. London, 1889–12 Oct 1924.
National Association of American Inventors. *World's Progress.* Jan 1878–May 1899.
  1878–1889: *American Inventor.*

APPENDIX B

Literature on Theatres: 1896
Compiled by William Paul Gerhard

The following bibliography appeared in *The American Architect and Building News*, 27 June 1896, 125-127. It appears to be unique among nineteenth century sources. Abbreviations, titles, and other contents are shown as presented in the original, however, bibliographic form has been modernized. A footnote to the original states: "The list given does not pretend to be complete, and the compiler will esteem it a favor, if interested readers will call his attention to any omissions or inaccuracies."

I. BOOKS – ENGLISH

Birkmire, Wm. H. *The Planning and Construction of American Theatres*. New York, 1896.

Buckle, James Geo. *Theatre Construction and Maintenance*. London, 1888.

Gerhard, Wm. Paul. *Theatre Fires and Panics, their Causes and Prevention*. New York, 1896.

Sachs, Edwin O., and Woodrow, Ernest A. E. *Modern Opera-houses and Theatres*. 3 Vols. Vol. I: London, May 1896.

Saunders. *Treatise on Theatres*. London, 17 . . (?).

Shaw, Capt. Eyre M. *Fire in Theatres*. 2nd Ed. London, 1889.

BOOKS – GERMAN

Handbuch d. Architektur. Theil III Bd.; Theil IV Bd.

Baukunde des Architekten. Bd. I. 2.; II.

Büsing, Prof. F. W. *Die Sicherheit in Theatern*. Bd. 6, Heft 2 des Handbuchs d. Hygiene. Jena, 1894.

Cavos, A. *Ueber die Einrichtung von Theater-Gebäuden*. Leipsic, 1849.

Doehring, W. *Handbuch des Feuer-Lösch-und-Rettungswesens*. Mit Atlas. Berlin, 1881.

Fischer, Herm. *Fortschritte der Architektur*. Heft 5.

_____. *Heizung Lüftung u. Beleuchtung der Theater*. Darmstadt, 1894.

_____. *Der Wieder Aufbau d. Stadt-Theaters zu Riga*. Riga, 1888.

Flech, Prof. D. H. *Ueber Flammensicherheit u. Darstellung flammensicherer. Gegenstände*. Dresden, 1882.

Fölsch, Aug. *Theater-Brände und die zur Verhütung derselben erforderlichen Schutzmassregeln.* Hamburg, 1878.

_____. *Ergänzungsheft dazu.* Hamburg, 1882.

_____. *Erinnerungen aus d. Leben eines Technikers.* – *Theater Brände.* Hamburg, 1889.

Gilardone, Franz. *Handbuch des Theatre-Lösch-und Rettungswesens.* 3 Vols. Strassburg und Hagenau; 1882, 1884.

_____. *Zum Brand der Komischen Oper in Paris.* Hagenau, 1887.

_____. *Der Theater-Brand zu Exeter.* Hagenau, 1888.

Hasenauer, Carl Freiherr von. *Hofburg-Theater, das k. k. in Wien.* 1889.

_____. *Hoftheater, das neue, zu Dresden.*

Hönig, Fritz. *Loeschen und Retten.* Köln, 1894.

Hude, H. v. d. und J. Hennicke. *Das Lessing-Theater in Berlin.* 1889.

Klasen, Ludwig. *Grundriss-vorbilder von Gebäuden aller Art.* Abth. VIII. Leipsic, 1884.

Landhaus. *Ueber Akustik und Katakustik der Theater.*

Langhaus, C. F. *Das Stadt-Theater in Leipzig.*

_____. *Das Victoria Theater in Berlin.*

Lindner, Dr. Gustav. *Das Feuer.* Brünn, 1881.

Lucae, R. *Das Opernhaus zu Frankfurt a. M. Herausgegeben von Giesenberg und Becker.* 1883.

March, Otto. *Das Städt. Spiel-und Festhaus zu Worms.* Berlin, 1890.

_____. *Das Stätische Spiel-und Festhaus zu Worms.* Vortrag, 1890.

Null, van der, und Siccardsburg. *Das k. k. Hof-Opernhaus in Wien.*

_____. *Erbaut von der Architekten. Opernhaus, das neue, in Wien.* 1879.

Runge, G. *Das neue Opernhaus* (Academy of Music). Philadelphia, 1882.

Schinkel, Karl Friedr. *Dekorationen auf den Königl. Hoftheatern zu Berlin.* 1874.

Semper, G. *Das Königl. Hoftheater in Dresden.* Brunswick, 1849.

_____. *Das (alte) Königl. Hof-Theater in Dresden.*

Staude, G. *Das Stadt-Theater zu Halle a. S.* 1886.

Staude, Gustav. *Das Stadt-Theater zu Halle.* Halle, a. S., 1886.

Strack, J. H. *Das alt-griechische Theater-Gebäude.* Potsdam, 1843.

Sturmhöfel, A. *Szene der Alten un Bühne der Neuzeit.* Berlin, 1889.

_____. *Akustik des Baumeisters.* Berlin, 1894.

Tietz, E. *Das Kroll'sche Etablissement in Berlin.*

Titz. *Das Wallner-Theater und das Viktoria-Theater in Berlin.*

Venerand, W. *Asbest und Feuerschutz.* Wien, 1886.

Weiseler, F. J. A. *Theater-Gebäude bei den Griechen und Römern.* Göttingen, 1851.

BOOKS – FRENCH

Chenevier, P. *L'Incendie de l'Opéra-Comique de Paris, et le Théàtre de Sureté*. Paris, 1888.

Constant, C. *Parallèle des Principaux Théâtres Modernes de l'Europe et des Machines Théâtrales*. Paris, 1820.

Moynet, Georges. *Trucs et Decors. – La Machinerie Théâtrale*. Paris (about 1892).

Moynet, M. J. *L'envers du Théâtre*. Paris, 1888.

Petit, Maxime. *Les Grande Incendies*. Paris, 1882.

BOOKS – ITALIAN

Daly et Davioud. *Les Théâtres de la Place du Châtelet*. Paris, 1874.

Donghi, Daniele. *Sulla Sicurezza dei Teatri in Caso d'Incendio*. Torino, 1888.

Garnier, Chas. *Le Nouvel Opéra de Paris*. Paris 1875–81.

Garnier. *Le Théâtre*. Paris, 1871.

Gosset, A. *Traité de la Construction des Théâtres*. Paris: Baudry & Co., 1886.

Nuitter. *Le Nouvel Opéra*. Paris: Librarie Hachette, G., 1875.

II. PAMPHLETS

Gerhard, Wm. Paul. *Theatre Fire Catastrophes and their Prevention*. New York, 1894.

———. *The Essential Conditions of Safety in Theatres*. New York, 1894.

———. *The Water-Service and Fire Protection of Theatres*. New York, 1894.

Hexamer, John C. *On the Prevention of Fires in Theatres. Journal of Franklin Institute*. August 1882.

———. *The Construction and Interior Arrangement of Buildings Designed to be Used as Theatres*. July 1892.

———. *Causes of Fire. Journal of Franklin Institute*. April, July, August, 1893.

Hexamer, John C. and others. *Report of Special Committee of the Franklin Institute on the Prevention of Fires in Theatres*. June 1883.

Sachs, Edwin O. *Urban Fire Protection*. London, 1895.

———. *Notes on Fire Brigades and Appliances of Continental Cities*. London, 1894.

Shaw, Eyre M. *Fire in Theatres*. First Edition. London, 1876.

*Report of the Committee on Theatres and Public Halls of the Citizens'
Association of Chicago.* I: January 1882; II: October 1883; III:
1887.

Young. *Theatre Panics and Their Cure.* London: Batsford, 1896.

VierteLJahrschrift der Weiner Freiw. Rettungsgesellscahft. Jan–Mar
1883. Vol. II, 1, 2, 3, enth. Denkschrift ueber Paniken in
Theatern.

Becker u. Giesenberg. *Das Opernhaus zu Frankfurt am Main.*

Boög, C. und v. Jonstorff, Hans Frh. v. Juptner. *Zur Sicherheit des
Lebens in due Theatern, mit besonderer, Berücksichtigung der
Theater-Brände.* Wien, 1882.

Fichtner, J. *Die Feuer-Sicherheit im Theater.* Striegau, 1882.

_____. *Theater-Brände und deren Verhütung.* Brünn, 1881.

Fockt, C. Th. *Der Brand des Ring-Theaters in Wien.* Wien, 1881.

Foelsch, Aug. *Ueber Theater Brände, u. ueber die für das neue
Opernhaus in Wien getroffenen Sicherheits-Massregeln.* Wien,
1870.

_____. *Der Ring-Theater-Prozess in Wien.* Wien, 1882.

Gilardone, Franz. *Die neuesten Erfahrungen auf d. Gebiet der Theater Sicherheits-Frage.* Hagenau, 1888.

_____. *Die Theater-Brände des Jahres.* 1888.

Jung, Ludwig. *Für Feuerwehren.* Viele Hefte.

_____. *Die Feuersicherheit in Oeffentlichen Gebäuden.* München,
1879.

Junk, D. V. *Das Theater-System der Gegenwart u. Zukunft.* Wien,
1884.

Patera, Ad. *Ueber Flammen-Schutzmittle.* Wien, 1871.

Prokop, Aug. *Die Sicherheit der Person im Theater, nebst einem Bei-
trag zur Theater Bau-Frage.* Brünn, 1882.

Richter, Heinr. *Die Feuer-Sicherheit der Theater.* Würtzburg, 1886.

Scholle, Friedr. *Ueber Theater Brände, daren Ursachen und
Verhtung.* Dresden, 1882.

_____. *Ueber Imprägnations-Verfahren als Schutzmassregel gegen
Feuersgefahr.* Dresden.

Dienstliche Anweisung für das Grossherz Hoftheater zu Wiemar.
Wiemar.

*Vorschlage des Nieder-Oesterreichischen Gewerbe-Vereins betreffend
die Sicherung von Theatern gegen Feuers-Gefahr.* Wien, 1882.

Stude. *Ein Mahnwort an Jedermann ueber Feuer-Sicherheit u.
Feuerschutz im Theater.* Brünn, 1882.

Ziembinski, Stanislaw. *Neue selbsthätige Feuer-Signal-Apparate,
und end Vorschlage z. Verhüten der Theater-Brände.* Krakau,
1882.

Veröffentl. der Deutschen Edison Gesellschaft. I. Das Edison-Glühlicht, u. seine Bedeutung für das Rettenswesen. Berlin, 1883.

Veröffentl. der Deutschen Edison Gesellschaft. II. Elektrische Beleuchtung von Theatern. Berlin, 1884.

Projekt einer Theater-Reform der Gesellschaft zur Herstellung zeitgemässer Theater "Asphaleia". Leipzig, 1882.

Brouardel, Dr. "La Mort dans les Théâtres," *Revue Sanitaire de la Provence.* No. 132–133, June 1889.

Chenevier, P. *La Question du feu dans les Théâtres.*

———. *Extinction des Incendies des Théâtres.*

———. *La Securitè des Spectateurs dans les Théâtres.*

———. *Reflexions sur l'Incendie de l'Opera-Comique.*

———. *L'Opera-Comique (Apres l'Indendie).*

———. *La Defense des Théâtres ACtuels Contre l'Indendie.*

Choquet, Docteur. *Les Incendies dans les Théâtres.* Paris, 1886.

Figuier. *L'Incendie dans les Théâtres.* 1881.

Lëgoyt, M. *Statistique des Incendies dans les Théâtres.* 1882.

Piccoli, D. V. *La Question du feu dans les Théâtres.* May, 1881.

Tripier, Dr. A. *Assainissment des Théâtres; Ventilation, Eclairage, Chauffage.* Paris, 1864.

———. *Sur la Ventil. et l'Eclairage des Salles de Spectacle.* Paris, 1864.

Vivien. *Suretè dans les Théâtres.*

ARTICLES IN JOURNALS AND MAGAZINES

1. "The Construction and Arrangement of Theatres." Report of a Committee appointed by the Austrian Society of Engineers and Architects, 1882.
2. "The Prevention of Fires in Theatres." Report of the Special Committee of the Franklin Institute, 1883. *American Architect*, 9 Jun 1883.
3. "Prevention of Fires." Report of the Committee of the Society of Arts, London, 1883. *American Architect*; 6, 23 Jun 1883.
4. R. G. "Theatre Fires." Four papers. *Fire and Water*, 1877.
5. J. A. F. "Theatre Fires and Remedies." Two papers. *American Architect*; 22 Oct, 12 Nov 1887.
6. Woodrow, E. A. E., Architect. "Theatre Construction." Four parts, *Inland Architect*, Aug–Oct 1890.
7. Woodrow, E. A. E. "Prevention and Extinction of Fires in Theatres." *Journal Society of Arts*, London, 18 April 1884.

8. Shean, Arthur W. C. "Fire, its Prevention and Extinction in Theatres." *Journal Society of Arts*, London, 18 Apr 1884.
9. Woodrow, E. A. E. "Prevention and Extinction of Fires in Theatres." *Journal Society of Arts*, 8 Jul 1892, Reprinted in *Building*, 20 Aug 1892.
10. Woodrow, E. A. E. "Theatrical Architecture." I–VI. *American Architect*; 10 Oct, 19 Dec 1891.
11. Woodrow, E. A. E. "Theatre Building Regulations." I–VII. *American Architect*; 16 Apr, Aug 1892.
12. Fox, John A. "American Dramatic Theatres." Five articles. *American Architect*, Jul–Sep 1879.
13. Percy Fitzgerald. "Scenic Illusion and Scenic Appliances." *Journal Society of Arts*, 18 Mar 1887.
14. Woodrow, E. A. E. "Theatres." Twenty-two articles. *American Architect*, 14 Apr 1884–Oct 1895.
15. Woodrow, E. A. E. "Theatres." Forty-seven articles. *Building News*, London, 15 Jul 1892–28 Dec 1894.
16. "Hygiene of the Stage." *The Stage*. London, Jul–Oct 1886.
17. Turner, Ernest. "The Sanitation of Theatres." Reprinted in *Building*, 24 Oct 1891.
18. Roth, W. E. "Hygiene of the Theatre." *American Architect*, 22 Oct 1887.
19. Birkmire, W. H. "The Planning and Construction of American Theatres." Twelve articles. *Building*, 13 Oct 1894–7 Mar 1896.
20. Gerhard, Wm. Paul. "The Essential Conditions of Safety in Theatres." *American Architect*; 23 Jun, 7, 14, 23 Jul 1894.
21. Sachs, Edwin O. "Some Suggestions as to Theatre Architecture." *Builder*, 15 Dec 1894.
22. Woodrow, E. A. E. "The Protection of Theatres from Fire." *Building News*, 27 Sep 1895.
23. Sachs, Edwin O. "The Safety of Theatre Audiences." *Building News*, 27 Sep 1895.
24. Sachs, E. O. "Modern Theatre Stages." *Engineering*, London. I–VIII; 17, 31 Jan, 14, 28 Feb, 13 Mar, 10, 24 Apr, 8 May [1896] (not yet concluded).
25. Woodrow, E. A. E. "Concert Halls and Assembly Rooms." I, *Building News*, 11 Oct 1895 (not yet concluded).
26. "Theatre Fire Catastrophes and their Prevention." *Scientific American Supplement*; 27 Oct, 3 Nov 1894; also *Fire and Water*, 1894.
27. "Water-supply and Fire Prevention of Theatres." *Fire and Water*, 1894.
28. "Some Recent Developments in theatre Planning." *Building News*, 25 Mar 1892.

29. "An Anniversary – the Ring Theatre Fire." *American Architect,* 23 Dec 1882.
30. Adler, Dankmar. "Paramount Requirements of a Large Opera-house." *Inland Architect and Building News,* Oct 1887.
    Cady, J. C. "Essential Features of a Large Opera-house." *Inland Architect and Building News,* Oct 1887.
31. Kobbé, Gustav. "Behind the Scenes of an Opera House." [*Scribner's Magazine,* Oct 1888, 435–454].
32. Sachs, Edwin O. "Fire Prevention." *Journal Society of Arts,* 7 Dec 1894.
33. Embden, Walter. "Theatres and Fireproof Construction." *Journal Society of Arts,* 27 Jan 1888.
34. Walters, Theodore. "Electric Stage Effects." *Electric Power,* May 1896.
35. Adler, Dankmar, Architect. "Theatre Building for American Cities." Two articles. *Engineering Magazine;* Aug, Sep 1894.
36. Sachs, Edwin O. "New Theatres at Berling and their Safety against Fire and Panic." *American Architect,* 19 May 1894.
37. Montgomery, C. S. "Bad Air in Theatres." *Engineering Magazine,* Vol. VIII, No. 2, May 1892.
38. Seddon, John P. "Theatre Ventilation." *Building News,* 15 Feb 1884.
39. "Fifth Avenue Theatre." *Scientific American,* Architects' and Builders' Edition, Mar–Jul 1891.
40. "Fifth Avenue Theatre." *Engineering Record,* Jul–Aug 1891.
41. "Theatre Machinery." *Frank Leslie's Monthly Magazine,* Feb 1895.
42. Gerhard, W. Paul, compiler. "Literature on Theatres." *American Architect,* Jul 1896.

IV. RULES AND REGULATIONS

Polizei-Verordnung betreffend Anlage u. innere Einrichtung von Theatern, Cicusgeb. u. öffend. Versammlungs-Räumen. Berlin, 1889.

Nachtrag dazu. Berlin, 1891.

Bestimmungen ueber die Bau-Art der von der Staats-Bau-Veraltung auszuf. Gebäude unter besonderer Berüchsichtigung der Verkers-Sicherheit. Berlin, 1892.

London County Council. *Metropolitan Building Acts.* Regulations made by Council, 9 Feb 1892, with respect to theatres.

Letter relating to Precautions against Fire, by the Lord Chamberlain, to theatre managers, 15 Feb 1864.

V. OFFICIAL REPORTS

Report from the Select Committee on "Theatrical Licenses and Regulations," together with the Proceedings of the Committee, Minutes of Evidence, Appendix and Index. London, 1866 (Blue Book).

Report from the Committee of the House of Commons on "Theatres." London, 1887 (Blue Book).

Report from the Select Committee on "Theatres and Places of Entertainment," together with the Proceedings of the Committee, Minutes of Evidence, Appendix and Index. (House of Commons Blue Book, 2 Jun 1892).

BIBLIOGRAPHY: 1989

Books

Barnheim, Alfred L. *The Business of the Theatre*. Rev. Ed. New York, 1964.

Birkmire, W. H. *The Planning and Construction of American Theatres*. New York, 1901.

Gorelik, Mordecai. *New Theatres for Old*. Binghamton, NY, 1940.

Hopkins, Albert A. *Magic*. New York, 1897.

Jennings, John J. *Theatrical and Circus Life*. Chicago, 1893.

Leverton, Garrett H. *The Production of Later Nineteenth Century American Drama: A Basis for Teaching*. Teachers' College, Columbia University, "Contributions to Education," No. 677. New York, 1936.

Moses, Montrose J. and John Mason Brown. *The American Theatre as Seen by its Critics, 1752-1934*. New York, 1934.

Poggi, Jack. *Theatre in America: the Impact of Economic Forces, 1870-1967*. Ithaca, NY, 1968.

Sachs, Edwin O. *Fires and Public Entertainments*. London, 1897.

United States Patent Office. *Collection of 83 Patents on Apparatus for Theatrical Illusions and Gymnastic Performances*. Washington, 1874-1901.

_____. *Collection of Patents on Apparatus for Producing Illusory Effects*. Washington, 1903-1909.

Vardac, A. Nicholas. *Stage to Screen: Theatrical Method from Garrick to Griffith*. Cambridge, MA, 1949.

Articles in Periodicals

"Art on the Stage," *Scientific American Supplement*, XII(1881) 4622.

"Asbestos Curtain, Terry's Theatre," *Engineer*, (London), 25 Nov 1887, 430.

"The 'Asphaleia' Stage at Buda-Pesth," *American Architect and Building News*, 19 Dec 1896, 97-100.

(Collapse of Theatre Seats, *American Architect and Building News*, 6 Aug 1892, 78.

(Competition for Theatre Designs), *American Architect and Building News*, 3 Apr 1897.

"The Construction and Arrangement of Theatres," Report of the Committee appointed by the Austrian Society of Engineers and Architects (Vienna), *American Architect and Building News*; 25 Mar, 8 Apr 1882; 138–140, 162–164.

Coolidge, J. R., Jr. "Notes upon the Architectural Works of Charles Garnier," *Architectural Review*, Sep 1898.

Corbould, William. "Stage Carpentry," *Work*, 21 Nov 1891–27 Feb 1892 (4 issues).

_____. "Stage Perspective," *Work*, 19–24 Sep 1891.

Crane, W. H. "Some Developments of the American Stage During the Past Fifty Years," *University of California Chronicle*, Apr 1913, 207.

"Electric Aids to the Drama," *Scientific American*, LIX(1880), 390–391.

"The Electric Light at the Adelphi Theatre," *Engineer* (London), 25 Jan 1889, 72–73.

"Electric Light at the Covent Garden Theatre," *Scientific American*, 30 Sep 1899, 211.

"The Electric Lighting of the Theatre at Earl's Court Exhibition," *Engineer* (London), 6 Nov 1896.

"The Electrical Manipulation of Theatrical Machinery," *Scientific American Supplement*, 7 Oct 1899, 19873.

"Electrical Notes," *Scientific American Supplement*, 8 Mar 1899, 19413.

"Electricity Behind the Stage," *Scientific American Supplement*, 3 Mar 1890, 11954–11955.

"Electricity in the Theatre," *Scientific American Supplement*, 10 Oct 1896, 17331–17332.

Emden, Walter. "Hydraulic Power for Working the Stage," Institution of Civil Engineers, *Proceedings* (London), 22 Apr 1888, 66.

_____. "Theatres," *Building News and Engineering Journal*, 23 Mar 1883, 349–352.

Ende, Max am. "Structural Ironwork in Theatres," *Engineer* (London), 1 Feb 1899, 94–95.

"Fireproof Scenery," *American Architect and Building News*, 6 Jan 1877, 7.

Fitzgerald, Percy. "On Scenic Illusion and Stage Appliances," *Journal of the Society of Arts*, 18 Mar 1887, 456–466.

"The Folly Theatre in Brooklyn," *Engineering Record*, 11 Aug 1900.

Gerhard, William Paul. "The Essential Conditions of Safety in Theatres," *American Architect and Building News*, 23 Jun–21 Jul 1894 (4 issues).

_____. "Water Service and Fire Protection," *Engineering News*, 21 Jun 1894, 518.

(Glasgow Theatre Fire), *American Architect and Building News*, 27 Apr 1895, 38–39.

Henderson, W. J. "Some New York Theatres," *Magazine of Art*, IX(1886), 401-407.

Hexamer, John C. "The Construction and Interior Arrangements of Theatres," *Building News and Engineering Journal*, 15 Jul 1892, 65-67.

Holmes, Charles Nevers. "The Park Theatre, New York," *Magazine of History* XXII(1916), 72-75.

"The Horse Race on the Stage," *Scientific American*, 25 Apr 1891, 263-264.

"How Theatres Should be Constructed," *American Architect and Building News*, 18 Jun 1892, 181-182.

"An Improved Theatre," *Building News and Engineering Journal*, 6 Jan 1882, 8.

Larson, Orville K. "A Commentary on the 'Historical Development of the Box Set' [by John H. McDowell]," *Theatre Annual*, XII(1954), 28-36.

Lathrop, George Parsons. "The Inside Working of the Theatre," *The Century Illustrated Monthly Magazine*, Jun 1898, 265-275.

Lautenschlaeger, Carl. "Theatrical Engineering Past and Present," *Scientific American Supplement*, 22 Jul 1905, 24686-24687, 24701-24703.

"Lautenschlaeger's New Revolving Stage," *Scientific American Supplement*, 29 Aug 1896, 17230-17231.

Logan, Olive. "The Secret Regions of the Stage," *Harper's New Monthly Magazine*, Mar 1874, 628-642.

McDowell, John H. "Historical Development of the Box Set," *Theatre Annual*, III(1945), 65-82.

"Modern Stage Mechanism," *Scientific American*, 7 Oct 1899, 232.

"Movable Theatre Stages," *Scientific American*, 5 Apr 1884, 209-210; *Scientific American Supplement*, 30 Aug 1884, 7210-7211.

"A New Way of Outlining Theatre Scenery," *American Architect and Building News*, 3 Mar 1877, 72.

"No Stage Door," *American Architect and Building News*, 6 Jan 1877, 7.

Pomeroy, W. H. "Effects on the Stage," *Home and Country*, Nov 1893, 1743-1754.

(Prussian Building Regulations for Theatres), *American Architect and Building News*, 28 May 1892 196.

(Revolving Stage at Munich Court Theatre), *American Architect and Building News*, 22 Aug 1896, 58.

"The Revolving Stage at the Munich Royal Residential and Court Theatre," *American Architect and Building News*, 12 Sep 1896, 83-84.

Sachs, Edwin O. "The Accident to the Drury Lane Stage," *Engineering* (London), 1 Oct 1897, 419–420.

_____ . "The Fire at the Iroquois Theatre, Chicago." British Fire Prevention Committee, *Publications*, No. 81.

_____ . "Modern Theatre Stages," *Engineering* (London), 17 Jan 1896–11 Jun 1897 (31 issues).

"Scenic World," *The Cornhill Magazine*, Mar 1886, 281–296.

Southern, Richard. "Trick-work in the English Nineteenth Century Theatre," *Life and Letters Today*, May 1939, 94–101.

Stonehouse, Augustus. "A Glance at New York Theatres," *Art Review*, Apr 1887, 6–8.

Sullivan, M. J. "The Temple of Electricity," *Electrical World*, 14 Nov 1891, 363–364.

Swanson, Wesley. "Wings and Backdrops: The Story of American Stage Scenery from the Beginnings to 1875," *Drama*, Oct 1927, 5–7ff.

"A Theatre Heated by Electricity," *American Architect and Building News*, 1 Jun 1895, 92.

"Theatre Regulations in New York," *Building News and Engineering Journal*, 5 Aug 1892, 195–196.

"Theatres and Population," *American Architect and Building News*, 22 Sep 1894, 112.

"Theatrical Machinery," *Engineer* (London), 25 Apr 1894, 311.

"Theatrical Machinery in the Paris Opera Housa," *Engineer* (London), 29 Feb 1884, 162–164.

"Ventilation of Theatres," *Building Age*, May 1899, 108.

Warington, Alphonse. "Theatrical Stage Arrangements and Machinery," *Builder*, 20 Apr 1861, 261.

Woodrow, Ernest A. E. "Theatre Building Regulations," *American Architect and Building News*, 16 Apr–20 Aug 1892 (7 issues).

_____ . "Theatres," *American Architect and Building News*, 14 Apr 1894–22 Feb 1896 (23 issues).

_____ . "Theatres," *Building News and Engineering Journal*, 15 Jul 1892–28 Dec 1894 (47 issues).

"Dressed for the Charade," frontispiece from *Peterson's Magazine*, February, 1885. Courtesy of the Margaret Woodbury Strong Museum.

COURTSHIP.—A CHARADE IN THREE ACTS.

ACT I.
COURT—

DRAMATIS PERSONÆ.

LORD CHIEF JUSTICE.   COUNSEL.
PRISONER (a Sailor).
EIGHT LADIES (his Wives).
JURYMEN, POLICEMEN, SPECTATORS, &c.

TIME—*Before supper-time.*

SCENE—*A Court of Justice. At back of Draw-ing-room the Lord Chief Justice's easy-chair,* and ottoman for Counsel. To the right, sofa for Jurymen. To the left, fire-screen for Prisoner's dock.

FLOURISH of splendidly imitated trumpets. Enter procession in following order: The USHER, holding the carpet-broom of office; His HONOR, robed in gorgeous dressing-gown, and wearing a magnificent wig of ermine victorine; the COUNSEL, carrying carpet-bags, holding briefs of music, and properly wigged with night-caps; the wretched SAILOR, who stands charged with the dreadful crime of polygamy, in the

close custody of the JAILOR, bearing the street-door key of office, and endeavoring to restrain his prisoner from dancing the hornpipe.*

As soon as Prisoner is safely secured behind fire-screen, he again breaks out in a hornpipe, when

. Enter the eight PLAINTIFFS (ladies whom the inconstant Prisoner has respectively mar-

ried in the several ports he has visited). They are natives of various countries, and dressed in their different national costumes.

At sight of the vile Sailor they are deeply moved, and intimate a strong desire to get at him. Enter JURYMEN, who are immediately packed into the sofa.

Counsel for prosecution, in the most electri-

* Unfortunately for the pantomimic art, the hornpipe is the only means left for proving that a gentleman in black continuations is a sailor.

fying dumb-show, proves, by pointing and frowning at Prisoner, who is still dancing, what a villain the man is. He shows the validity of each marriage by putting an imaginary ring on his third finger; and having referred to the case of "LACHI DAREM—in RE DON GIOVANNI," *Italian Duets,* Vol. II., demands, by a thump on the ottoman, that the scoundrel should be punished with the utmost rigor of the law.

Judge, putting on the black hat, proceeds to pass sentence of death on the wretched Prisoner, who evinces the utmost callousness by doing the split in the hornpipe.

The wives no sooner hear their joint husband's doom than an affectionate rush is made towards him, which the wretched man perceiving, he seeks safety in flight.

TABLEAU.

Charade instructions for the word "Courtship." *Godey's Lady's Book and Magazine,* December 1854, pages 517 and 518. Courtesy of the Margaret Woodbury Strong Museum.

47

ACT II.
—SHIP.

DRAMATIS PERSONÆ.
CAPTAIN, SAILORS, PASSENGERS, &c.

SCENE—*The deck of that fast-sailing craft, the Front Drawing-room.*

ENTER CAPTAIN, with noble cocked-hat, made out of yesterday's *Times*, and hair-brushes

for epaulettes. He shouts through a set of quadrilles, when

Enter several tight lads, who proceed to the music-stool to heave at the capstan and weigh

the imaginary anchor; whilst others pulley-oi at the larboard bell-rope to let out gallant main-

top ceiling. Two more brave boys take the wheel, and, by means of the arm-chair, steer the room beautifully.

PASSENGERS on after-ottoman now begin, by wild gesticulations—the turning up of eyes, and the sudden application of handkerchiefs—to intimate that they have passed the Nore Light; whilst others, leaning over the backs of their chairs, implore their neighbors, in the most affecting pantomime, to throw them overboard.

Enter STEWARD with basins, at which the

passengers make a simultaneous rush. He also enables several poor creatures, who are walking about in the most extraordinary manner, and rolling from side to side of drawing-room, to reach their berths.

Presently a fearful storm is supposed to arise. The Passengers, binding life-preservers of comforters round their waists, jump hurriedly from their berths, and, springing over the sides of the ship, strike out for the door, where *exeunt omnes.*

———

ACT III.
COURTSHIP.

DRAMATIS PERSONÆ.
OLD FATHER. HIS DAUGHTER. HER LOVER. RETAINERS, LAWYER, &c. &c.

SCENE—*Apartment in mansion of Old Father.*

ENTER DAUGHTER, who shows, by pressing her side and swinging about, that she is deeply in love. She commences laying a table for two, and, having set down a lovely round of cold

bandbox, she again expresses her fondest devotion for one of the knives and forks.

Sweet plaintive sounds of a splendidly-executed whistle are heard without. She claps her hands, and

Enter LOVER in full uniform of the new police, richly silvered with chalk. He glances

anxiously at the cold round of bandbox, and then gives vent to the wildest movements of joy. They advance to table, and feast commences. Just as he has helped himself to the

Charade instructions for the word "Courtship." *Godey's Lady's Book and Magazine,* December 1854, pages 517 and 518. Courtesy of the Margaret Woodbury Strong Museum.

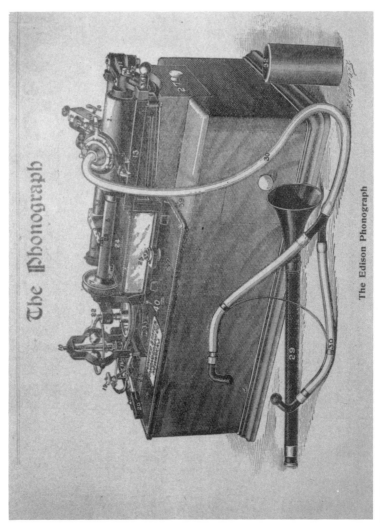

The Edison phonograph. *The Phonoscope,* February 1897, December 15, 1896, page 1. Science & Technology/Annex, The New York Public Library.

A picture projecting device. *The Phonoscope*, July 1897, page 10. Science & Technology/ Annex, The New York Public Library.

A Phonograph Studio.

Where Voices of Noted Artists are Stored.

SARAH BERNHARDT LISTENING TO THE BETTINI
MICRO-PHONOGRAPH.

Sarah Bernhardt listening to a Bettini micro-phonograph. *The Phono-scope*, December 15, 1896, page 1. Science & Technology/Annex, The New York Public Library.

MISS FARRAR LISTENING TO "I'M AFRAID TO COME HOME IN THE DARK," BY CLARICE VANCE.

Geraldine Farrar listening to a Victor machine, *The Talking Picture World*, April 15, 1908, page 52. Science & Technology/Annex, The New York Public Library.

Cover of the December 1906 *The Columbia Record.* Rodgers & Hammerstein Archive of recorded Sound, The New York Public Library.

Political cartoons from *The Talking Picture World*, August 15, 1908, page 33. Science & Technology/Annex, The New York Public Library.

The Columbia Record

This is one of the methods by which Columbia Graphophones and Records are advertised in St. Petersburg.

Two interesting pictures are here given, illustrating the enterprise of our agents in Japan. The Columbia Phonograph Company was given an important place in the Exposition recently held in Tokio, where Columbia Graphophones and our Japanese Records have taken a strong hold on the people. The photograph from which these illustrations were made were sent here by one of our exclusive agents for Japan, Mr. Kingoro Ezawa. The picture on the left shows the building in which our exhibit is being held. The one on the right shows the bo oth.

Promotional events for the Columbia Phonograph Company in Russia and Japan. *The Columbia Record*, September 1907, page 6. Rodgers & Hammerstein Archive of Recorded Sound, The New York Public Library.

Advertisement for a recording by "Uncle Josh," a popular "rube" character comic. *The Columbia Record,* July 1910, page 10. Rodgers & Hammerstein Archive of Recorded Sound, The New York Public Library.

Costumes designed by Homer Conant for *The Passing Show of 1916 (l)* "Phoebe Snow from Buffalo;" *(r)* "Your Auto Ought to Get Girls." The Shubert Archive.

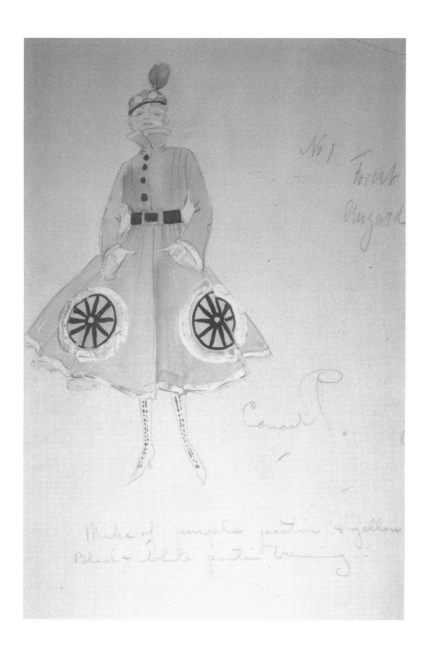

EX-LAX MANUFACTURING CO.

MAKERS OF

EX-LAX CHOCOLATE
EX-LAX "FIGS"
EX-LAX Gum

SOLE DISTRIBUTORS
OF

YUM
FOR HEADACHE

CABLE ADDRESS
EXLAX NEWYORK

431-443 ATLANTIC AVENUE
BROOKLYN, N.Y.

JUNE
Twenty-Second
1926.

Shubert Productions,
Purchasing Department,
231 West 45th Street,
New York, N. Y.

Gentlemen:-

We are planning a sampling
campaign on EX-LAX FIGS covering the entire
theatrical district (sample enclosed
herewith); and we would ask you for the
courtesy of permitting one of our girls to
stand outside of your theaters for a few
hours, during the week of June 28th.

For this courtesy, we will
send you a case of EX-LAX TOILET PAPER
(100 Rolls) with the compliments of our
company.

We are enclosing self-addressed
stamped envelope for your reply.

Very truly yours,

EX-LAX MANUFACTURING CO.

MK:CW.

Secretary.

An example of correspondence between a manufacturer and the Shubert Productions purchasing office. The Shubert Archive.

POPULAR ENTERTAINMENT IN THE TRADES: A CASE STUDY OF THE *NEW YORK CLIPPER* AND THE *NEW YORK DRAMATIC MIRROR*

by Stephen M. Vallillo

While researching the early career of George M. Cohan, I extensively consulted the *New York Dramatic Mirror* and the *New York Clipper*, two of the most valuable resources for information on the late nineteenth and early twentieth century American theatre. The two periodicals were show business trade papers – the *Variety*'s of their day, if you will (*Variety*, in fact, bought out the *Clipper*) – which documented the business of the theatre: the comings and goings of theatrical personalities, the routes of touring productions, reviews of shows in New York and on the road.

Started in 1853, the *Clipper* covered theatrical and sporting amusements until 1924. In addition to its coverage of sports, including baseball and racing, the *Clipper* printed reviews, casting notices, advertisements by and for performers, interviews with and articles on performers, lists of attractions in New York theatres and on the road, and columns on circus, vaudeville, minstrelsy, and the legitimate theatre. In its first few months, the *Clipper* was primarily devoted to sports, but soon a column called "City Amusements," which listed information about theatre and music, was added. In 1856 the paper started a "Theatrical Directory," listing the whereabouts of performers and playbills from theatres across the country. By 1859, the editors announced that they wished to make the paper useful to the profession as well as general readers and again requested information from performers

STEPHEN M. VALLILLO earned a doctorate in Performance Studies from New York University with his dissertation on George M. Cohan as a director. He has published scholarly articles in journals and books and works as a stage manager.

and managers. By this time the *Clipper* had become a trade paper for theatre and other amusements, which still included sports. In 1880, an editor, looking back over the papers early years, described it as "the weekly record of the stage, growing from an insignificant beginning to a history of cyclopedic dimensions."[1]

The first issue of The *New York Mirror*, which later became the *New York Dramatic Mirror*, was published on January 4, 1879. Its cover featured an engraving of Tony Pastor and advertisements of the bills of some theatres as well as individual performers. Subtitled "A Reflex of the Dramatic Events of the Week," the *Mirror*, unlike the *Clipper*, was solely devoted to the theatre. It included a correspondence section, which grew to be quite extensive, featuring reports on the dramatic events in other cities, reviews of New York productions, advertisements, route listings for touring productions and an editorial page.

The paper soon became identified with its editor, Harrison Grey Fiske, whose name first appeared on the masthead on July 17, 1880 although he had been editing it for some time previously. The *Mirror* advocated a number of what it considered reforms for the profession including the Actors' Fund (a theatrical charity), amendment of the copyright laws for dramatic works, and the playing of the national anthem before all theatrical performances.

The paper featured the writing of Nym Crinkle (the pseudonym of A. C. Wheeler) as well as special features including a series of essays on the theatre by notable writers, scholars and performers, including Dion Boucicault, Brander Matthews and Helena Modjeska. Its interest was not only literary. In 1893, a series on American scenic painters was printed and three years later the paper gave its readers a ten-part look behind the theatre curtains in a series entitled "The Making of the Theatre."

Unlike the *Clipper*, the focus of the *Dramatic Mirror* was restricted to the legitimate theatre until 1895 when a vaudeville department was added. Reviews of vaudeville acts were printed, along with the playing dates of performers and a column with information about vaudevillians.[2]

The *New York Dramatic Mirror* continued until April 1922, two years before the *Clipper* also ceased. By then, newer theatrical trade papers, including *Variety* and *Billboard*, had taken over the field. However the two papers continue to provide rich documentation of the late nineteenth and early twentieth century American theatre.

My purpose is not to describe these two newspapers, which has been done in greater detail elsewhere, but to demonstrate how they could be used in a specific research project. I found both papers invaluable when researching the early career of George M. Cohan in popular entertainment. I initially assembled a chronology of his career between his birth in 1878 and 1901, his first appearance in a full-length musical comedy in a New York theatre, from his autobiography and the two published biographies, as well as several theses and a dissertation. These sources generally agreed on the dates of his various engagements, they all followed the outline Cohan provided in his autobiography. I then decided to get supporting detail from the trade papers to fill out this chronology.

In his book, Cohan describes how, in late 1896 when he considered breaking up the family act and giving up his own performing career due to lack of bookings, his family was recruited at the last minute to perform their vaudeville act at Hyde and Behman's theatre in Brooklyn. Rushing to the theatre, they had to open the show, but still made a great hit with the audience. Audiences loved them, the managers immediately moved them to a better spot on the bill and they were booked to return as headliners. Soon they were hired for Hyde's travelling vaudeville show, which supposedly ensured their success and catapulted them into the top rank of variety performers. Surely such success would have been reported in the trade papers. When I found no mention of the Four Cohan even appearing in Brooklyn on that date, I began searching the trade papers in the months immediately preceding and following that date. Finally I found a mention of the Four Cohan's on the bill at Hyde and Behman's during the week of January 20, 1896.[3] There was no evidence of the dramatic success Cohan describes, and the family must not have generated too much interest in the profession because by the beginning of February they had joined the cast of *The Jester*, a touring play with music.

I soon realized that the generally accepted chronology was inaccurate. Clearly Cohan the playwright also dramatized his life, so I began a systematic search of the two trade papers week by week between about 1888 and 1900 to obtain a true picture of his early career.

The Cohan family worked in all forms of popular entertainment. Jerry Cohan, George's father, wrote plays, skits and songs, and performed in vaudeville, minstrel shows, travelling play companies. He occasionally formed his own companies. In 1887, the entire family joined the company of *On the Trail, or Daniel Boone the Pioneer*, a play by Charles Gayler which showcased Captain Jack Crawford, a well-known Indian scout. George's parents, Jerry and Nellie, performed and his sister Josie had her first role, Lilly Boone. The dates and title of the play were verified by advertisements in the *Clipper*, and information about Josie Cohan was included in an article about her written several years later.[4]

Cohan's first starring role was Henry Peck, the title character in a touring production of *Peck's Bad Boy*. In his autobiography, Cohan described his success and how he felt "that guy Booth had nothing on me."[5] The reviews in the *Dramatic Mirror* support this interpretation to some extent. One said his portrayal was "Clever and caught the house," but another noted only that "the Cohan girls, Georgie, Josie and Nellie, met with an enthusiastic welcome.[6] The company travelled across the east coast and as far west as Minneapolis before ending up in New England in April 1892. On April 9, the Four Cohans ran an ad in the *Clipper* stating "Close season with *Peck's Bad Boy* company April 9. Strong cards for any company, dramatic or specialty. Can be engaged at once or for next season."[7]

The next major engagement that Cohan described in his autobiography was an appearance at Robinson's Theatre in Buffalo, at Thanksgiving 1892, originally scheduled for a single week but extended until the following summer as the family gave performances ranging from sketches, specialties and dances to full length melodramas. The *Clipper* and the *Mirror* confirm their appearances at Robinson's theatres in Buffalo and Rochester. The Cohan Comedy Company is first included on the Rochester theatre's bill in the December 3, 1892 issue of the *Clipper*, and their billing varied throughout the next six months. Their first mention from Buffalo (December 10) listed Jerry Cohan as well as Josie and George Cohan. In several issues the Cohans, as a family, were mentioned and in the May 27 and June 3, 1893 issues, Josie Cohan received first billing. The family was not named in several issues but in those weeks they may have been performing with the theatre's stock company, which was frequently mentioned. The March 18 *Clipper* cites a performance of *The Molly Maguires*, a play written by Jerry Cohan, done by the stock company. In an ad the following September, the Cohan's heralded their success: "Went to Buffalo November '92, for 2 weeks and stayed until June, '93 under the management of M. S. Robinson." The ad also includes short quotes from reviews, in Buffalo newspapers, of Josie Cohan as the star attraction. These excerpts mentioned some of her dances ("Modern Hether"[sic] and Spanish tambo) and noted that she had been appearing with a stock company in several previous weeks.[8]

That fall, the Four Cohans finally reached New York. B. F. Keith, who had hired Jerry Cohan in the past, reopened the Union Square Theatre as a continuous vaudeville house in mid-

September, and after two weeks each as Keith's theatres in Boston and Philadelphia, the Four Cohans made their New York debut on October 2.[9] The theatre listings in the *New York Clipper* indicate that, in Boston and Philadelphia, the Cohans performed a four-act (a four-person sketch) one week and their individual specialties the next. In New York, Keith had them perform individually. According to his autobiography, George was upset because he felt that the four-act was sure to be successful. And he exploded when he found he had been given the worst place on the bill, the opening spot. His act, "The Lively Bootblack," was a failure all week.[10]

Despite George's disappointment, the other Cohans did quite well. Josie was immediately hired by the Imperial Theatre for the following week, and according to an advertisement the family ran in the *Clipper*, they were all booked for an early return to Keith's in their new act. Josie was a success at the Imperial, and appeared on the bill there for the weeks of October 30 and November 6 as well.[11] George's inactivity, while his sister worked, make him feel dissatisfied; in his book, he exaggerated the month and a half without work into many long months of unemployment for the family, with Josie as their sole support.[12] However, for newcomers to New York City, the Cohans were actually doing well. They played Huber and Gebhardt's Casino (also known as Zipp's Casino) in Brooklyn as a four-act from November 20 through December 2. And the following week, they finally performed at Keith's Union Square in their act "Goggle's Doll House."[13]

In 1984, Josie appeared in several New York theatres and clubs, and the family presented their four-act at venues including Proctor's, Keith's theatres in Boston and Philadelphia, and New York's Central Opera House. George was beginning to develop as a performer, and he was commended by the *Clipper* for his "character change work."[14]

In the fall, the Cohans joined Gus Williams's production of his play *April Fool*. Williams was a popular German dialect comedian, who had toured the play the previous year. George, who played the low comedy juvenile, wrote that he offended Williams by offering to rewrite the play. He also chafed under the comedian's direction. Cohan obeyed him in rehearsal, but at the first performance, he played the first act in his own way. "Instead of the 'silly kid' character I was supposed to be and had been rehearsed to play, I twisted the thing around to a flip, impudent, dashing young juvenile in a low-comedy make-up."[15] Only quick apologies, forced out of him by his family, kept him from being fired. He also wrote that, after thirty-five miserable weeks, the family was fired following another argument with the business manager. However, the *Clipper* indicates that the Cohans stayed with the show until it closed in Cincinnati on January 19, 1895.[16]

After *April Fool* closed, the Cohans performed in several other touring shows, including M. S. Robinson's *On the Road*, a musical farce starring Lydia Yeamans-Titus about show business, which included "Six Great Specialists."[17] George and Josie were both singled out in reviews for their dancing. *On the Road* closed a month later in Cincinnati due to a weak script and troubles with the star. The *Clipper* printed the manager's explanation of his troubles with Mrs. Titus in the World Players column, including this description of the first performance in Detroit:

> In the first act some gamin in the gallery hooted Mrs. Titus. She took umbrage at this and left the stage. No persuasion of mine, my manager, or the local manager, Mr. Stair, would induce her to go on again that evening. This, of course, killed our business for the week.[18]

Robinson went on to describe further problems leading to his star fainting at the end of a performance and the demise of the production. This sort of detailed inside information often appeared in the trade papers.

The Cohans advertised for variety work again, mentioning their abilities: "Single Specialties, Dual Sketches and Entire 'Four' Act. All Are Expert Character Actors."[19] In November they were back on the Keith circuit, and on November 25 they presented their revised version of "Goggle's Doll House" at the Union Square Theatre. By this time the sketch had become the Four Cohans' trademark, but they kept improving it. Reviews described Josie's new "Bicycle Dancing Novelty" – she rode in on a bicycle and sang a cycling song – and George's "Automatic Dance," which started slowly and sped up as it went along. They still finished, however, with their "Unrivalled DANCING DOLLS."[20] Their reputation was still growing, as the *Clipper* suggested: "The Four Cohans returned to friends made through previous work, and renewed their success in an emphatic manner."[31] They continued to perform their improved sketch in variety theatres through the end of the year.

In September of 1896, the Four Cohans joined Richard Hyde's vaudeville show. Advertisements in the *Clipper* provide an interesting perspective on the show. The Cohan's advertisements said they were added to strengthen the show during the first two weeks, a charge vehemently denied by Hyde on his own ad the following week. They remained with the show until mid-January, when they resigned. (Cohan claimed that he left because of an argument with Hyde about billing. Their ads may be evidence of this.)[22]

Two incidents reported in the trade papers during the Hyde tour demonstrate Cohan's continuing development. In mid-November, while the company was performing at the Chicago Opera House, the Four Cohans introduced a new sketch, "Goggle's Wife," by George M. Cohan.[23] This twenty-minute sketch, which later became known as "The Professor's Wife," was based on Jerry Cohan's old sketch. It added new action and business, but shrewdly still concluded with the famous dancing dolls specialty. The new play helped the Cohans to become more popular than ever, but more importantly, it marked the first time the family had performed one of George's pieces. From this time forward, he wrote all of the Cohans' material.

In December, while Hyde's company was performing in New York City, two of Mrs. Cohan's sisters died within one day of each other. Her husband and daughter joined her at the double funeral in Rhode Island, while George performed alone. He scored a success with a monologue and his eccentric dancing, and, by the end of 1896, he had become good enough as a dancer and comedian to hold an audience by himself.[24]

After the Cohans left Hyde's Comedians, they headed out to California for a six-week engagement on the Orpheum circuit in Los Angeles and San Francisco. While in Los Angeles, on March 8, 1897, they introduced a new sketch by George, "Money to Burn."[25] After a summer vacation, they premiered their new act at Tony Pastor's on September 13. The new sketch firmly cemented their position as vaudeville headliners, as a November 1897 article in the *New York Dramatic Mirror* suggests.

> The Cohans, up to the end of last season, have been known as a good quartette, who gave satisfaction in every bill in which they appeared, but were scarcely to be considered as headliners. This season they turned up with a brand new thirty-minute sketch, called Money to Burn, which was written by George M., the youngest of the Cohans. Within forty-eight hours after they had produced the new comedietta offers of splendid time at an increased salary began to flow in.
>
> The first manager who secured them billed them as stars, and this state of things has prevailed ever since, while their salary has been increasing by leaps and bounds.[26]

The Four Cohans' status as vaudeville headliners is confirmed by two items from the trade papers late in 1898. The *Clipper* mentioned, in one of its columns, that in September the Cohans had been offered a large salary for one performance at the Vanderbilt mansion in Newport. Unfortunately, they had to turn down the offer because they were already booked to perform in New Haven. And in December, the Cohans played Sunday concerts at Weber and Fields' Music Hall for four weeks in a row. Weber and Fields made the travel arrangements to and from the family's other engagements and paid all expenses. As the *New York Dramatic Mirror* phrased it, "This is evidence that they have made an extraordinary impression on the *blase* patrons of the Broadway Music Hall."[27]

For the next two and a half years the Four Cohans maintained their position as stars by headlining several vaudeville road companies. In December 1897, the family performed with the Vesta Tilley Vaudeville Company, organized by Weber and Fields. In October of 1898, the Cohans joined Harry Williams' Own Company, and performed "Running for Office" in major cities in the east and midwest until the following March. The following September, they starred in the Behman show, and again crisscrossed the country for over a year.

On February 24, 1900, the Four Cohans, now heading the Behman Show, presented George's new sketch, "The Governor's Son." It was a typical Cohan piece, and according to the *Dramatic Mirror*, "everything goes with a snap and vim that is decidedly refreshing." Cohan was praised for his acting as well. His character was "free from the exaggeration which he has indulged in heretofore, and he played with an ease of manner that surprised everyone."[28]

Behman's production of a three-act version of *The Governor's Son*, in Hartford, Connecticut on February 11, 1901, marked the Four Cohans' departure from vaudeville and their arrival on the legitimate musical comedy stage. While some vaudeville performers continued to use Cohan's sketches well into the first decade of the twentieth century, the Cohan family stayed on the Broadway stage (or on tour with their Broadway shows) for the rest of their careers. Except for a special engagement in Chicago during the week of August 4, 1902 ("for a salary of THREE THOUSAND DOLLARS ($3,000.00), being the Largest Weekly Salary Ever Paid to Any Act in the World"), the Four Cohans never performed in vaudeville again.[29]

Although George M. Cohan became one of America's most pop-

ular and renowned performers, he and his family were not especially well-known during the 1880's and early 1890's. Not until
1897 did they become vaudeville headliners and they did not
become Broadway stars until the early 1900's. However, it is still
possible to trace their routes and find evidence of their performances, their employment status and their careers before they
became stars in the two theatrical trade papers. The *New York
Dramatic Mirror* and the *New York Clipper* provide information
about the performances of the Four Cohans – and countless other
performers – in a number of different popular entertainment
forms including vaudeville, touring plays and musicals and even a
Wild West show. Clearly these two trade papers, which are widely
available on microfilm, are invaluable to scholars.

NOTES

[1] In addition to the newspaper itself, information about the *Clipper* is available
in "The 'Cyclopedic Dimensions' of the *New York Clipper*," by Virginia
Christ-Janer, *Bulletin of the New York Public Library*, June 1966, pp.
347–355.

[2] Information about the *New York Dramatic Mirror* is found in an article called
"The Story of the Mirror 1879–1899," in the Christmas 1899 issue of the
Mirror.

[3] The Four Cohans were listed in the reviews of Hyde and Behman's in the
January 20, 1896 issue of both the *Clipper*, p. 744, and the *Dramatic
Mirror*, p. 20. The "Variety and Minstrelsy" column of the same issue of the
Clipper (p. 742) mentioned that the Cohans were presenting "their revised
version of 'Goggles Doll House' [their vaudeville sketch] this week at Hyde
and Behman's Brooklyn Theatre.

[4] *New York Clipper*, advertisements on January 21, 1888, p. 728, and September 3, 1887, p. 388 (this casting advertisement called the play *On the Trail,
or Daniel Boone the Avenger*); "Josie Cohan," October 7, 1893, p. 490.

[5] George M. Cohan, *Twenty Years on Broadway: and the Years It Took to Get
There* (New York: Harper and Brothers Publishers, 1924), p. 23.

[6] *New York Dramatic Mirror*, November 28, 1891, p. 9; January 23, 1892, p.
11.

[7] *New York Clipper*, April 9, 1892, p. 79.

[8] Consult the listings for Buffalo and Rochester in the New York State section
of the New York *Clipper* from December 3, 1892 through June 10, 1893 for
information about the Cohans' performances at Robinson's theatres. Their
ad appeared September 9, 1893, p. 439.

[9] *New York Clipper*, "Boston," September 9, 1893. p. 429; "Boston," September
16, 1893, p. 448; "Philadelphia," September 23, 1893, p. 463; "Philadelphia," September 30, 1893, p. 481; "Union Square Theatre," October 7,
1893, p. 498.

[10] Cohan, *Twenty Years*, pp. 61, 67.

11*New York Clipper*, "Imperial Theatre," October 14, 1893, p. 514, November 4, 1893, p. 562; November 11, 1893, p. 578; ad in October 14, 1893, p. 523.

12Cohan, *Twenty Years*, pp. 73-76, 85-86, 105-109.

13*New York Clipper*, "Huber and Gebhardt's Theatre," November 25, 1893, p. 610; December 2, 1893, p. 626; "Keith's Union Square Theatre," December 9, 1893, p. 643.

14"Central Opera House Music Hall," *New York Clipper*, June 16, 1894, p. 230.

15Cohan, *Twenty Years*, p. 128.

16"Cincinnati," *New York Clipper*, January 26, 1895, p. 748.

17Ad for *On the Road*, *New York Clipper*, June 29, 1895, p. 269.

18"Detroit," *New York Dramatic Mirror*, September 21, 1895, p. 4. "World Players," *New York Clipper*, October 12, 1895, p. 502.

19Ad in *New York Clipper*, October 12, 1895, p. 513.

20Ad in *New York Clipper*, November 30, 1895, p. 622. "Keith's Union Square Theatre," *New York Dramatic Mirror*, December 7, 1895, p. 19.

21"Keith's Union Square Theatre," *New York Clipper*, November 30, 1895, p. 616.

22Ads in the *New York Clipper*, September 12, 1896, p. 447, and September 19, 1896, p. 463. Cohan, *Twenty Years*, p. 170.

23"Variety and Minstrelsy," *New York Clipper*, November 28, 1896, p. 615.

24"Miner's Eighth Avenue Theatre," *New York Clipper*, December 18, 1896, p. 668.

25"Vaudeville and Minstrel," *New York Clipper*, March 27, 1897, p. 56.

26"The Four Cohans," *New York Dramatic Mirror*, November 13, 1897, p. 18.

27"Vaudeville and Minstrel," *New York Clipper*, September 17, 1898, p. 476. *New York Dramatic Mirror*, December 17, 1898, p. 20.

28"Proctor's Fifth Avenue," *New York Dramatic Mirror*, June 9, 1900, p. 16.

29Ad in the *New York Dramatic Mirror*, August 9, 1902, p. 6.

SOUND RECORDING PERIODICALS—1890-1929

by Sara Velez

It was in 1877 that Thomas A. Edison first demonstrated his early talking machine, filing for a patent, on Dec. 24, 1877, for the "first phonograph to be built exclusively for the purpose of sound recording and reproduction at will."[1] He received his patent on Feb. 19, 1878, for a tin-foil phonograph which played as its first recording, Edison reciting: "Mary had a little lamb . . ."

An article heralding Edison's early work on the phonograph first appeared in the Nov. 17, 1877 issue of *Scientific American*, a journal whose editor was a friend of Thomas Edison, and which was to publish many other articles on the phonograph. Frank Mott, in his *A History of American magazines 1885-1905*, states that "*The Scientific American* continued to be the leading popular exponent of mechanical development and invention in the country."[2] Also in his book, Mott discusses a magazine called: "*Science*, which had a predecessor that had been founded on July 3, 1880, by Thomas A. Edison and edited by John Michels. It was rather heavy, being composed mainly of papers read before scientific associations . . . Alexander Graham Bell bought it . . . but let it lapse with the number for Dec. 31, 1881."[3]

In the May-June 1878 issue of the *North American Review*, Edison speaks of uses for the phonograph such as: "Letter writing and dictation; records of books, as read by elocutionists; educational purposes, for teaching languages and elocution; musical and entertainment records; family album of voices; toys, musical boxes; annunciators for clocks, etc.; advertising; preserving voices

SARA VELEZ is conservation officer and librarian in charge of print acquisition for the Rodgers & Hammerstein Archives of Recorded Sound, The New York Public Library. She has a B.A. in Comparative Literature from City College and an M.L.S. from Columbia University.

of the great."⁴ In their book, *From Tin Foil to Stereo*, Oliver Read and Walter L. Welch state that in the early days of the phonograph, there were very few musicians or music critics who had the farsight to see the great opportunities the phonograph offered for musical education including the preservation of the great voices and unique vocal styles of the period. They speak favorably of Compton Mackenzie who founded the English publication, *The Gramophone*, in 1923, stating: "Sir Compton Mackenzie is perhaps better known as a novelist, but he was also the first writer to effectively arouse public interest in the latent potential of the phonograph (or gramophone) in the creation of a recorded musical culture."⁵

Notwithstanding certain early reservations regarding the use of the phonograph, news of Edison's invention began to spread rapidly around the world. Even in countries as far distant as Russia and Colombia, South America, articles and journals began to appear in the late 1800's and early 1900's. In Russia, in 1878, three articles dealing with the phonograph appeared in the following journals: "Eshche o govoriashchei mashine ili fonografe Edissona," (*Svet*, no. 6); "Fonograf," (*Tekhnicheskiĭ sbornik*, nos. 5–6; "Fonograf, govoriashchaĭa mashina," (*Zhurnal dliĭa vsekh*, T. 2). In 1894, an article on Thomas Edison appeared in the *Repertio Colombiano*, from Bogotá, Colombia. Also, by 1902, Russia had a magazine devoted to the gramophone entitled: *Grammofon i fonograf*, to be shortly followed by *Grammofonnyĭ mir*, *Grammofonnaĭa zhisn'*, *Novosti grammofona*, *Svet i zvuk*, and others.

In the United States, *The Phonogram* appeared in 1891 and *The Phonoscope* in 1896. With regard to the latter, Oliver Read and Walter L. Welch, in *From Tin Foil to Stereo*, note that *The Phonoscope* was: "the first independent publication to be devoted primarily to the phonograph field."⁶ From Berlin, Germany, in 1900, came the *Phonographische Zeitschrift*, an organ dedicated to the phonograph industry. Also, around 1900, a monthly magazine appeared in Milan, Italy, entitled: *Rivista fonografica italiana*.

Early grammophone magazines from England were *The Phonogram*, which appeared in 1891, *Sound Wave*, 1906, and *Talking Machine News*, 1906. In France, *Bulletin phonographique et cinématographique* appeared in 1899 and *Machines parlantes & radio* appeared in 1919.

Turn of the century gramophone magazines serve as an interesting chronicle of the entertainment tastes of the times. One can find record listings and reviews for many of the popular entertainments of the late 1800's and early 1900's. There are listings of band favorites, both military and otherwise, played by bands from the U.S.A., England, France, Germany, Russia, etc. Other orchestral favorites, both classical and popular, including much music from operas, operettas, and other musical shows, are featured. Banjo duets, minstrel songs, gospel songs, and whistling solos were particular favorites of this period, as were rural comedy acts such as Uncle Josh & his "Weathersby's Laughing Stories." Other comedy acts as well as variegated vaudeville routines were very popular and widely recorded. There was much vocal music recorded in the way of solos, duets, quartets, etc. which covered the range of operatic arias, concert songs, and popular ballads. Recordings featuring bells, with orchestral accompaniment, were featured, as were recordings of political speeches, which were often used to galvanize political gatherings. Another example of early recordings being used to influence or instruct large gatherings were the gospel songs that were played at evangelical street meetings, which proved very successful in drawing crowds to the meetings. Russian monks used gramophone recordings in their monasteries to improve their singing techniques. Recordings were also used in the schools to provide rhythms for physical drills, marches, assemblies, parades etc.

Many of these early gramophone publications contain finely illustrated interviews with the leading personalities of the times. They also contain valuable technical material regarding the history and development of the early talking machines. In these early magazines, one can trace the rapid growth and expansion of the gramophone industry, by noting the various articles dealing with the many record production plants that opened around the world.

During the late 1800's and early 1900's, there were other publications that contained references to early gramophone activities, though they may not have been devoted primarily to that subject. Some American journals were: *Scientific American* (1845-), *Electrical World* (1885-), *American Machinist* (1877-), *North American Review* (1815-), and the *Journal of the Franklin Institute* (1826-). From England, publications such as *Electrician* (1862-), *Electrical Review* (1872-), *Musical opinion and musical trades review* (1877-), and *Nature* (1870-) also contained articles dealing with the early phonograph. From Berlin, Germany, *Elektrotechnische Zeitschrift*, which began in 1880, contained similar references. The above listed publications, *Scientific American* to *Elektrotechnische Zeitschrift*, can be found in The New York Public Library, 42nd St. & 5th Ave., except for *Musical opinion and musical trades review*, which can be found in The New York Public Library, Music Division of the Performing Arts Library at Lincoln Center. Publications from France which contained papers on the gramophone, talking machines etc. were: *L'Illustration: journal universel* (1843-), *Les Inventions illustrées: sciences, industrie, finance* (1899-), *La Nature: revue des sciences et de leurs applications aux arts et à l'industrie* (1873-), *La Science et la vie: magazine des sciences et de leurs applications à la vie moderne* (1913-), *La Science illustrée* (1887-), and *Science pour tous: revue populaire de vulgarisation scientifique* (1856-). *L'Illustration*, *La Nature*, and *La Science et la vie* (only 1940's issues), can also be found at The New York Public Library, 42nd St. & 5th Ave. Nineteenth and early twentieth century Russian publications that contained references to early talking machines were: *Zhurnal noveĭshikh otkrytiĭ i izobreteniĭ* (1896-), *Zapiski russkogo tekhnicheskogo obshchestva* (1867-), *Nauka i zabava* (1893-), *Niva: il. zhurnal lit., politiki i sobr. zhizn'* (1870-), *Ogonek: khudozhestv.-lit. zhurnal* (1899-), *Elektrichestvo* (1880-) *Elektrichestvo i zhisn'* (1910-), *Elektrotekhnik* (1897-), *Elektrotekhnicheskiĭ vestnik* (1894-).

Newspapers such as *The New York Times* contained many articles on the early gramophone industry in the late 1800's, as did to a lesser degree, papers such as: *New York Sun, Brooklyn Eagle, Boston Herald, Pittsburgh Leader*, and the *Washington Star*.

In the United States, the library which appears to have the largest collection of early sound recording publications is The New York Public Library: Rodgers & Hammerstein Archives of Recorded Sound, Science and Technology Division and Music Division. Other libraries which have smaller collections are the Library of Congress, Washington, D. C.; Yale University (Historical Sound Recordings Collection), New Haven, Connecticut; Stanford University, Stanford, California. All of these collections are open to the public. It would be wise to call the institutions first before going there, to ascertain visiting hours, as some of them, such as Yale and Stanford, only have hours from 1 to 5, on week days, and due to limited facilities, need to make appointments in advance to insure that there will be room available.

I have compiled a listing of early sound recording periodicals from 1890 to 1929. Included in the bibliography are some publications that were still in print after 1929, but began prior to that date. The listing is international in scope, and encompasses house organs of record companies such as Edison, Victor and Columbia, as well as independently produced publications. The periodicals appear in alphabetical order. Dates, country of publication, frequency, publisher, title variants and content annotations are given whenever possible. The holdings of assorted libraries and archives are listed, preceded by Library of Congress National Union Catalog location symbols, when applicable. Following the holdings information, are the institutions' call numbers when given.

LC NATIONAL UNION CATALOG LOCATION SYMBOLS

CSt: Stanford University Libraries, Stanford, California
CtY: Yale University, New Haven, Connecticut
    Historical Sound Recordings Collection [HSR]
    Music Library [YML]
DLC: Library of Congress, Washington, D.C.
NN: The New York Public Library, New York City
    Annex, 521 West 43rd St. [Annex]
    General Research Division, 42nd St. & Fifth Ave. [GRD]
    Performing Arts Research Center (PARC), Lincoln Center
        PARC-Music Division (PMU]
        PARC-Rodgers and Hammerstein Archives of Recorded Sound [PRH]
    Science and Technology Research Center, 42nd St. & Fifth Ave. [STC]
ONCG: National Library of Canada, Ottawa, Ontario [Music Division]

I would like to thank the following individuals and institutions for their kind assistance in the compilation of this bibliography: Gary-Gabriel Gisondi, Rodgers & Hammerstein Archives of Recorded Sound, The New York Public Library-whose publication, *Sound recordings periodicals, a preliminary union catalog of pre-LP-related holdings in member libraries of the Associated Audio Archives*, was a great source of information for this project; Donald McCormick, Rodgers & Hammerstein Archives of Recorded Sound, The New York Public Library; Richard Warren and his staff, Yale University, Historical Sound Recordings Collection; General Research Division and the Annex, The New York Public Library; Detroit Public Library; National Library of Canada, Music Division; National Archives of Canada, Moving Image and Sound Archives; Vancouver Public Library; National Film & Sound Archive, Canberra, Australia; National Library of Australia; The British Library, National Sound Archive; The British Library, Bibliographical Information Service; Staatliches Institut für Musikforschung Preussischer Kulturbeisitz, Berlin; Staatsbibliothek Preussischer Kulturbesitz, Berlin; Bibliothèque Nationale, Département de la Phonothèque Nationale et de l'Audiovisuel, Paris; M. E. Saltykov-Shchedrin State

Public Library, Leningrad, USSR; Lenin State Public Library, Moscow, USSR.

NOTES

[1]Read, Oliver & Walter L. Welch. *From Tin Foil to Stereo.* (Indiana: Howard W. Sams & Co., 1977, p. 10)

[2]Mott, Frank. *A History of American Magazines* 1885-1905. (Cambridge, Mass.: Harvard University Press, 1957, p. 320)

[3]Ibid., p. 307.

[4]Read, Oliver & Walter L. Welch. p. 412.

[5]Ibid, p. xvi.

[6]Ibid., p. 64.

EARLY PHONOGRAPH PUBLICATIONS

1. *Along Broadway*: the Edison musical magazine. 1916-? Orange, N. J.: Thomas A. Edison, inc. Monthly. Includes illustrated articles on popular artists, musical articles and record reviews. NN: v. 1-12, Apr. 1916-Apr. 1922. [PRH: *LA (Edison, Thomas A., inc. Along Broadway)]

2. *Arts Phoniques*: la première revue d'art uniquement consacrée au phonographe. 1928-1929? Paris, France. Monthly. Guy de Sarnez, directeur. Carl Vica, editor in chief. Bibliothèque Nationale, Département de la Phonothèque Nationale et de l'Audiovisuel. Paris, France.: No. 1, février 1928, no. 2, mars 1928, no. 5, juin 1928, no. 10, novembre-décembre 1928, no.II, janvier 1929. [B.N., Phonothèque Per 73]

3. *Australasian Phonograph Monthly*. 1925-27. Sydney, Australia. Publisher: Count L. de Noskowski. Includes record reviews of such labels as Apex, Brunswick, Columbia, H.M.V., Parlophone, Edison Diamond Discs and Polydors, and gramophone articles. The Phonograph Society of N.S.W., Sydney, Australia.: the entire run of the magazine is being reprinted serially in the quarterly journal of the Society.

4. *Better Selling Bulletin*. 1921?-1923? U.S.A. Continued by: *Better Letters Bulletin*. Weekly. Both bulletins include letters to Penn-Victor dealers from the Penn Phonograph Co. ONCG: Feb 4, 1921-Sept. 23, 1923. (incomplete) [Manuscript Collection: Harold D. Smith Papers]

5. *Billboard*. Cincinnati, etc. Monthly (Nov. 1894-May 1900); weekly (June 1900-date) Title varies: *Billboard Music Week* (v. 73-74, 1961-1962) Material in the earliest years of the publication dealt with theatrical news, including columns highlighting the current theatrical activities and performers from Berlin, London and Paris. Also included articles on vaudeville, carnivals, fairs, tent shows, poultry shows, skating rink news, film advertisements, film reviews and some musical news. Articles dealing with sound recordings and record reviews do not appear until the 1930's. CSt: v. 24-72, 1912-60 [809.205 ARS] NN: v. 1 to date, Nov. 1894-present. [PMU: all back issues on microfilm in *ZAN-*M 63; current year also on file in PRH: *LA (Billboard)]

6. *Bulletin Phonographique et cinématographique*. 1899?-1900? Paris, France. Bi-monthly. M. Siry, director. Later titles: *Les Inventions et les Industries Nouvelles, Bibliothèque des Inventions et des Industries Nouvelles*. Bibliothèque Nationale, Département de la Phonothèque

Nationale et de l'Audiovisuel. Paris, France.: No. 1, 1899?–1900?
[B.N. Imprimés 4 5603]
7. *Canadian Music and Trades Journal.* 1900–? Canada. v. 1, no. 6,
Nov. 1900–v. 10, no. 3, Apr. 1905. Irregular. (Incomplete) Title
changed to: *Canadian Music Trades Journal.* v. 13, no. 3, Aug.
1912; no. 7, Dec. 1912. v. 13, no. 8, Jan. 1913–v. 33, no. 8, Jan.
1933. (Complete except for Sept. 1921 & Dec. 1931). Title changed
to: *Canadian Music and Radio Trades.* V. 1, no. 8, Jan. 1931.
ONCG: [Music Division]
8. *The Columbia Record.* 1903–? New York. Columbia Phonograph
Co. Monthly. Includes news of various early graphophone dealers
and stores, technical articles, interviews with performers, brief
record reviews etc.
CtY: v. 2, no. 1–10; v. 3–5, no. 4, 8–9; v. 6, no. 11; v. 7, no. 3, 8–9,
11; v. 14, no. [12] (Dec. 1916). [HSR]
DLC: Feb., Mar. 1907; Mar. 1908; Mar.–Apr. 1909.
NN: v. 2–15,; Jan. 1904–May 1917. [PRH: *LA (Columbia Phonograph Company, inc. Columbia Record)]
9. *The Columbia Salesman.* 1906?–?
CtY: v. 2, no. 2; v. 5, no. 3; Oct. 1907, Feb. 1908. (Electrostatic
copies) [HSR]
10. *Disques.* 1929–62. Paris, France. Monthly. Simone-Aimée Lam-
bour et Maurice Cloche, directors. Includes listings of new recordings with company and label nos., artists, composers, record
reviews, recording articles.
Bibliothèque Nationale, Département de la Phonothèque
Nationale et de L'Audiovisuel. Paris, France: No. 1, juin 1929 et
no. 2, octobre 1929. [B.N. Imprimésl Jo 46 688]
NN: No. 26, Feb. 1937–No. 130, 1962 (incomplete). [PRH: *LA
(Disques); *ZAN-*MP 10 (Nos. 47–56, 1939–Mar./Apr. 1940 on
microfilm)]
11. *Duo-Art Music.* 1913?–1930? New York. Aeolian Co. Monthly.
Detroit Public Library, Music & Performing Arts Dept.: v. 10–v.
17, no. 1, Oct. 1923–no. 3, Dec. 1930 (incomplete).
12. *Edison Amberola Monthly.* SEE: *Edison Phonograph Monthly.*
13. *Edison Diamond Points.* 1915–? Orange, New Jersey. Monthly.
"Devoted entirely to the Edison Diamond Disc Phonograph and
Record business." Includes industry articles, music articles, capsule record reviews.
CtY: v. 1, no. 2–4, 6–9; v. 2, no. 2. [HSR]
NN: v. 1–7, Dec. 1915–Jan. 1922 [PRH: *LA (Edison, Thomas A.,
inc. Edison diamond points)]
14. *Edison Phonograph Monthly.* 1903–? Orange, New Jersey.
Monthly. Published for trade use only by the National Phono-

graph Co. Includes advance listings of new Edison molded records with artists and label nos., sales information, lists of jobbers of phonographs and records, from the United States and Canada. British Library. National Sound Archive. 1903-1912. [Reprints of original edition] CtY: v. 10, no. 9; v. 12, no. 4-12; v. 13, no. 2-4, 6, 12; v. 14, no. 1, 4-5, 9, 11; v. 15, no. 1. [HSR] DLC: (Details not reported) [ML 155.5E35] National Library of Australia, Canberra: v. 1-v. 7, 1903-1909. [S 789.9105 EDI] NN: v. 1-17, Mar. 1903-Dec. 1918; Feb. 1919-Jan./Feb. 1922 [PRH: *LA (Edison, Thomas A., inc. Edison Amberola monthly)] ONCG: v. 1-11, 1903-1913. [Music Division]

15. *L'édition Musicale Vivante*; études critiques de la musique enregistrée: disques, rouleaux perforés, etc. 1927-? Paris, France. Monthly. Superseded by: *Sélection de la vie artistique* (1934-1935). Emil Willermoz, director. Includes listings of new record releases, record reviews, musical articles etc.
Bibliothèque Nationale, Département de la Phonothèque Nationale et de I'Audiovisuel. Paris, France: No. 1, décembre 1927-no. 80, nov. 1934. [B.N. Imprimés 4 V 11129]
DLC: 1927-34. [ML5.S365]
NN: Dec. 1927-Dec. 1930. [PRH: *LA]

16. *Grammofon I Fonograf.* 1902-1906. Saint Petersburg, Russia. Tipografiia N.N. Klobukova. Weekly. Includes listings of newly released recordings, historical surveys of the phonograph/gramophone industry, illustrated biographical articles of important persons in the gramophone industry, illustrated articles of early Russian gramophone apparatus, including factories, libretti of popular recorded songs and arias, illustrated vignettes of well known artists. In 1904, became a monthly publication. Title changed in 1905-1906 to *Svet I Zvuk*; in Aug.-Sept. 1906 to *Grammofon I Fotografiia*.
CtY: 1902-1904. [HSR]
Gosudarstvennaia Ordena Lenina Biblioteka SSSR imeni V. I. Lenina. [Lenin State Public Library] Moscow, USSR: Nos. 1-3, 1902; Nos. 1-17, 1903; Nos. 1-12, 1904; Nos. 1-2, 1906.
Gosudarstvennaia Ordena Trudovogo Krasnogo Znameni Publichnaia Biblioteka imeni M. E. Saltykova-Shchedrina. [M. E. Saltykov-Shchedrin State Public Library] Leningrad, USSR: Nos. 1-3, 1902; Nos. 1-17, 1903; Nos. 1-12, 1904; Nos. 1-12, 1905; Nos. 1-6, 1906.

17. *Grammofon I Fonograf.* 1907-? Serpukhov (Moscow District).

Gosudarstvennaíā Ordena Lenina Biblioteka SSSR imeni V. I. Lenina. [Lenin State Public Library] Moscow, USSR: No. 1, 1907.
Gosudarstvennaíā Ordena Trudovogo Krasnogo Znameni Publichnaíā Biblioteka imeni M. E. Saltykova-Schchedrina. [M. E. Saltykov-Shchedrin State Public Library] Leningrad, USSR: No. 1, December 1907.

18. *Grammofon I Fotografiíā.* See: *Grammofon I Fonograf.* Saint Petersburg.

19. *Grammofonnaíā Zhizn.'* [Grammophone life] 1911–1912. Moscow, Russia. bi-weekly. Fabrikant i optovik. Includes grammophone advertisements, listings of new recordings, illustrated technical and historical articles, concert, opera and operetta reviews, illustrated articles about popular artists, capsule record reviews. CtY: nos. 1–17, 20–31; 1911–1912. [HSR]
Gosudarstvennaíā Ordena Lenina Biblioteka SSSR imeni V. I. Lenina. [Lenin State Public Library] Moscow, USSR: Nos. 1–17, 1911; Nos. 20–31, 1912.
Gosudarstvennaíā Ordena Trudovogo Krasnogo Znameni Publichnaíā Biblioteka imeni M. E. Saltykova-Shchedrina. [M. E. Saltykov-Shchedrin State Public Library] Leningrad, USSR: Nos. 1–18, 1911; Nos. 1/19–31, 1912.

20. *Grammofonnyĭ mir/die Grammophon–Welt.* [Grammophone world] 1910–1917. Saint Petersburg, Russia. Monthly. Pervi spetsialnyĭ zhurnal posviashennyĭ interesam grammofonnoĭ promishlennosti i torgovli. Includes grammophone advertisements, articles in German and Russian, capsule record reviews, technical articles, illustrated sketches of artists. Cty: 1910–1912, 1914–1917. [HSR]
Gosudarstvennaíā Ordena Lenina Biblioteka SSR imeni V. I. Lenina. [Lenin State Public Library] Moscow, USSR: Nos. 2–12, 1910; Nos. 1–23, 1911; Nos. 1–20, 1912; Nos. 1–20, 1913; Nos. 1–14, 1914; Nos. 1–8, 1915; Nos. 1–12, 1916; Nos. 1–2, 6–8, 1917.
Gosudarstvennaíā Ordena Trudovogo Krasnogo Znameni Publichnaíā Biblioteka imeni M. E. Saltykova-Shchedrina. [M. E. Saltykov-Shchedrin State Public Library] Leningrad, USSR: Nos. 1–12, 1910; Nos. 1–22/23, 1911; Nos. 1–20, 1912; Nos. 1–20, 1913; Nos. 1–13/14, 1914; Nos. 1–5, 7–8, 1915; Nos. 1–12, 1916; Nos. 1–2, 6/7–8, 1917.

21. *The Gramophone.* 1923–. London, England. Monthly. Title varies: v. 7, no. 84–v. 8, no. 89, *The Radio Gramophone.* Includes music articles, listings of recommended recordings, record society articles and comprehensive record reviews.
Australian National Film & Sound Archive, Canberra, Sydney and

Melbourne offices: v. 5, no. 10, 1928-v. 62, no. 742, 1984.
(Complete)
Australian National Library, Canberra: v. 5, no. 10-v. 60, no. 717,
1928-1983. 1928-1943 held at MUS. [S 789.9 GRA]
British Library. National Sound Archive. 1923-date.
Cty: V. 9, nos. 99, 102. 104-105, 107; v. 10, nos. 110, 115; v. 12,
nos. 141-142, 144; v. 13, nos. 147-148, 151; v. 14, nos. 158, 160,
164, 166, 168; v. 15, nos. 169-175, 177-178, 180; v. 16, nos.
181-182, 185-186; v. 20, nos. 230, 238; v. 23-35, nos. 416, 419; v.
36, nos. 422-429; v. 37, nos. 433, 436-443; Aug., Nov. 1931; Jan-
.-Feb., Apr., July, Dec. 1932; Feb.-Mar., May, Aug.-Sept., Dec.
1935; July, Sept. 1936; Jan., Mar., May-Dec. 1937; Feb.-Mar.,
May-July, Oct.-Nov. 1938; July 1942; Mar. 1943; June 1945-Jan.,
Apr., July 1958-Feb., June, Sept. 1959-Apr. 1960. [HSR] v.
38-date; June 1960-date. [YML]
CSt: v. 4, nos. 1-8, 10-12; v. 12, no. 139; v. 13, nos. 153-156; v. 15,
nos. 169-175; v. 17, nos. 194-202, 204; v. 18, nos. 210,212; v. 19,
no. 223; v. 23, nos. 275-v. 24, 30, no. 360; v. 38, no. 455; v. 39, nos.
457-464, 466; v. 40, nos. 478, 480-date; June 1926-Jan., Mar-
.-May 1927; Dec. 1934; Feb.-May 1936; June-Dec. 1937; July
1939-Mar., May-Nov. 1940; Jan.-Dec. 1941; Apr. 1946-May
1947; May 1953-Apr., June 1961-Jan., Mar. 1962; May
1963-date.
DLC: Complete to date. [ML5. G65]
NN: Complete to date. [PRH: *LA (Gramophone)]
NSyU: v. 1-14; 16-date; Apr. 1923-May 1937; June 1938-date.
State Library of Victoria, Melbourne: v. 7, no. 73-v. 60, no. 719,
June 1929-Apr. 1983. [AOF 789.9 G76]
Vancouver Public Library. Vancouver, British Columbia. v. 3,
June 1925; v. 9, May 1932; v. 14, June 1936; v. 19, May 1942; v. 22,
June 1944-May 1945; v. 24, Mar. 1947-date.

22. *Gramophone & Talking Machine News*; a musical paper for all.
1908?-1928? London, England. Monthly. Includes articles on
recording artists, listings of new recordings with company and
label numbers, technical articles with illustrations, opera synop-
ses, record reviews.
NN: v. 17-22, nos. 417B-458B, July 1925-Dec. 1928. (incomplete)
Lacking: v. 17, nos. 418, 420; v. 18, nos. 423-434; v. 20, no. 455.
[PRH: *LA (Gramophone & talking machine news)]

23. *De Gramophoon Revue.* 1929-1933. Amsterdam, The Nether-
lands. Monthly. Absorbed by: *Schijven Schouw.* Published by
A.J.G. Strengholt en Allert de Lange. Een gids voor iederen
gramophoon-bezitter. Includes articles on popular recording artists, illustrated technical articles, listings of recordings with label

numbers from different companies, record reviews, both pop and classical.
NN: Microfilm: jaarg. 1, nr. 5-jaarg. 4, nr. 11; oct. 1929–Apr. 1933 (incomplete). Lacking: jaarg. 1, nr. 6–7, 10–11,; jaarg. 2, nr. 1, 8; jaarg. 3, nr. 5. [PRH: *ZAN-*MP 12]

24. *Kultur und Schallplatte.* 1929–? Berlin, Germany. Monthly. "Mitteilungen der Carl Lindström A.G., Kultur Abteilung." Includes music articles, record releases and record reviews.
DLC: Complete (1929–?) [ML5.K91]
NN: Jahrg. 1–2, Heft 10/11; Juli 1929–Mai 1931. [PRH: *LA (Lindstrom, Carl, A.G. Kultur and Schallplatte)]

25. *Listener in.* 1925?–? Melbourne, Australia. Monthly. Adgar H. Baillie, United Propriety Ltd. "The wireless journal of Australia." Australian National Film & Sound Archive, Canberra, Sydney and Melbourne offices. v. 1, no. 14, 1925–v. 16, no. 49. (incomplete)

26. *Machines Parlantes & Radio.* 1929–1939. Paris, France. Monthly. Office Général de la Musique. "Ancienne Revue des Machines Parlantes." Earlier title: *Revue des Machines Parlantes* (1919–Sept. 1929). Absorbed in Sept. 1939 by *Musique et Instruments.* Includes technical articles with diagrams, historical articles, listings of new releases giving titles, composers, performers, record companies and label numbers (including companies such as: Pathe, Odeon, Decca, Ideal, Ultraphone, Parlophone, Cristal, Lutin etc.).
NN: année 15–21, nos. 157–236, Jan. 1933–Juil./août 1939. [PRH: *LA (Machines parlantes & radio)]

27. *Music Lovers' Phonograph Monthly Review.* 1926–32. Boston, Mass. Monthly. The Phonograph Publishing Co., Inc. "An American magazine for amateurs interested in phonographic music and its development – only American magazine of its kind." Title varies: Oct. 1926–June 1927, Oct. 1930–Mar. 1932, *The Phonograph Monthly Review.* Superseded by: *Music Lover's Guide.* Includes technical articles with illustrations, articles on recording personages, the recording industry, comprehensive record reviews, phonograph societies' reports, listings of new releases with company and label numbers.
British Library. National Sound Archive. 1927–1932. (incomplete)
CSt; v. 1–6 (incomplete). Lacking v. 4, nos. 1–10; v. 5, nos. 4, 10; v. 6, nos. 2, 4–6. [ML 156.P974 ARS]
DLC: Complete. [ML1.P5]
NN: v. 1–6, Oct. 1926–Sept. 1931. Complete. [PRH: *LA (Music lovers' phonograph monthly review)]
ONCG [Music Division]: v. 1, nos. 1–3, 4, 5, 7, 9; Oct.–Dec. 1926,

Jan., Feb., 1927, Apr. 1927, June 1927; v. 1, no. 10, July 1927–v. 4, no. [12], Sept. 1930; Oct 1930–Dec. 1931; Mar. 1932.

28. *The Music Seller Reference Book.* 1927–? London, England. Annual. Evan Bros., Limited. "Records and music issued . . ." Includes factors of gramophone records (topographical), addresses of record manufacturers, alphabetical index to separate numbers of operas and oratorios, alphabetical listings of gramophone records with title, artist, record company and label number, music publisher, addresses of music publishers, listing of published sheet music and classified index of manufacturers and suppliers.
NN: 1927–1936. [PRH: *L (Music seller reference book)]

29. *Musique*: revue d'histoire, de critique, d'esthétique et d'informations musicales. 1927–1930? Paris, France. Monthly. Robert Lyon, director. Marc Pincherlé, editor in chief. Includes music articles, phonograph articles, book reviews, record reviews, concert reviews etc.
Bibliothèque Nationale, Département de la Phonothèque Nationale et de I'audiovisuel. Paris, France: No. 1, 1927–mars 1930. [B.N. Imprimés 4 V 10246]
NN: Année 1–3, Oct. 1927–mars 1930. [PMU: *MA (Musique)]

30. *Musique–Adresses*: annuaire français de la facture instrumentale, de L'édition musicale et des industries qui s'y rattachent. 1913–? Paris, France. Annual. Auguste Bosc, director. Title variant: *Annuaire O. G. M.* (after 1933).
Bibliothèque Nationale, Département de la Phonothèque Nationale et de L'Audiovisuel. Paris, France: 1913, 1914. [B.N. Imprimés 8 V 36385]
NN: 1913–1914, 1919–1925/26, 1928–1931, 1934, 1937–1939, 1941, 1954. [PMU: *MAD (Musique-Adresses-Universel)]

31. *Musique et Instruments*: revue générale de l'industrie et du commerce de la musique, des machines parlantes et de la radio. 1911–1984? Paris, France. weekly, bi-monthly. Auguste Bosc, director. Later title: *Musique et Radio.* Includes phonograph articles, listings of new recordings with company and label nos., artist, composer, musical articles, record reviews.
Bibliothèque Nationale, Département de la Phonothèque Nationale et de L'Audiovisuel. Paris, France: No. 1, 1911–. (incomplete) [B.N. Musique Vma 462]
NN: juillet 1923, no. 174, fév. 1924–no. 360, sept./oct. 1939; no. 488, 1952–1980. [PMU: *MA (Musique et instruments)]

32. *Muzykal'noe ekho.* 1914. Vil'na, Lithuania. Organ, posviashchennyĭ grammofonnoĭ promyshlennosti.
Gosudarstvennaïa Ordena Lenina Biblioteka SSSR imeni V. I.

Lenina. [Lenin State Public Library] Moscow, USSR: Nos. 1–5, 1914.
Gosudarstvennaĩā Ordena Trudovogo Krasnogo Znameni Publichnaia Biblioteka imeni M. E. Saltykova-Shchedrina. [M. E. Saltykov-Shchedrin State Public Library] Leningrad, USSR: Nos. 1–4/5, 1914.

33. *The New Phonogram.* 1904–? Orange, New Jersey, Monthly. The National Phonograph Co. Title varies: from Nov. 12–July 1914, the title read: *The Phonogram.* Includes listings of new Edison records with label numbers, artists and capsule reviews, phonograph cartoons and poems.
NN: v. 1, no. 1, July 1904–v. 11, no. 7, July 1914. [PRH: *LC ED. 4 Mus. Res.]

34. *Novosti Grammofona.* [Grammophone news] 1907–1908. St. Petersburg, Russia. Monthly. Includes Fonotipia record listings with label numbers, artists and repertoire, illustrated technical articles, illustrated vignettes of artists, libretti of recorded songs, arias etc., gramophone advertisements.
CtY: 1907–1908 (incomplete), [HSR]
Gosudarstvennaĩā Ordena Lenina Biblioteka SSSR imeni V. I. Lenina. [Lenin State Public Library] Moscow, USSR: Nos. 1,3, 5–9, 1907; Nos. 1–3, 1908.
Gosudarstvennaĩā Ordena Trudovogo Krasnogo Znameni Publichnaĩā Biblioteka imeni M. E. Saltykova-Shchedrina. [M. E. Saltykov-Shchedrin State Public Library] Leningrad, USSR: Nos. 1–9, 1907; Nos. 1–3, 1908.

35. *Ofitsial'nye Izvestiĩā Aktsionernogo Obshchestva Grammofon.* [Grammophone Co. news] 1908–1910. Moscow, Russia. Monthly. Title changed to: *Pishushchiĭ Amur I Grammofonnye Novosti* in 1910. Includes listings of recommended and best new recordings, articles on the grammophone industry, Zonophone news, small record reviews, articles dealing with grammophone libraries, Grammophone Co. news from around the world, humorous grammphone cartoons.
CtY: 1908–1910. [HSR]
Gosudarstvennaĩā Ordena Lenina Biblioteka SSSR imeni V. I. Lenina. [Lenin State Public Library] Moscow, USSR: Nos. 1–13, 1908/1909; Nos. 14–21, 1910.
Gosudarstvennaĩā Ordena Trudovogo Krasnogo Znameni Publichnaĩā Biblioteka imeni M. E. Saltykova-Shchedrina. [M. E. Saltykov-Shchedrin State Public Library] Leningrad, USSR: Nos. 1, 2–7, 9–13, 1908/1909; Nos. 14–21, 1910.

36. *Le Phono.* 1928–? Paris, France. Weekly.
Bibliothèque Nationale, Département de la Phonothèque

Nationale et de L'Audiovisuel. Paris, France: No. 1, décembre 1928-No. 9, février 1929. [B.N. Imprimés Jo 41206]

37. *Phono-Ciné-Gazette*; revue illustrée des questions intéressant le phonographe, le gramophone. 1905-1908? Paris, France. Bimonthly. Edmond Benoit Levy, director.
Bibliothèque Nationale, Département de la Phonothèque Nationale et de L'Audiovisuel. Paris, France: No. 1, avril 1905. [B.N. Imprimés Fol V 4959; until 1908]

38. *Phono-Magazine*. 1928-? Paris, France. Monthly.
No. 1, 1928-? No holding in the Bibliothèque Nationale. Title only listed in the *Annuaire de la Presse et de la Publicité* of 1929.

39. *Phono-Revue*. 1929-? Paris, France. Monthly.
No. 1, 1929-? No holding in the Bibliothèque Nationale. Title only listed in the *Annuaire de la Presse et de la Publicité* of 1929.

40. *Phono-Radio-Musique; Radiophonie, Phonographie, Télévision.* 1920?-1937? Paris, France. Monthly. Organe de la Chambre Syndicale de L'Industrie et du Commerce français des Machines Parlantes. J. M. Gilbert, director.
Bibliothèque Nationale, Département de la Phonothèque Nationale et de L'Audiovisuel. Paris, France: (No. 1, 1920?-1937?) Août 1924 (IV, no. 8), juillet 1926 (VI, no. 7), 1928 (whole year) [B.N. Imprimés Jo 63 220] 1933- [B.N. Phonothèque Per 71]

41. *The Phonogram*; a monthly journal devoted to the science of sound and recording of speech. 1893-? London, England. Monthly. The Phonogram Co., Ltd. Includes articles on the development of the phonograph and how to work it, lists of famous voices recorded by the phonograph, the uses put to the phonograph by actors and actresses etc.
NN: v. 1, nos. 1-3, May-July 1893. (Reproduction) [PRH: *LA (The Phonogram)]

42. *Phonogram*; printed monthly for those interested in phones, graphs, grams & scopes. "Devoted to the arts of recording and reproducing sound." 1900-1902. New York. Monthly. H. Shattuck. Includes gramophone riddles, poems, cartoons, articles dealing with various uses for the phonograph, listings of Edison concert records with label nos., including spoken word, songs sung in French, Italian, Yiddish, Latin, Swedish etc., historical articles (example: "the story of the phonograph. History: ancient, medieval and modern"), articles on popular theatrical artists.
NN: v. 1-6, no. 2, May 1900-Dec. 1902. Complete on microfilm. [PRH: *ZAN-*MP 4]

43. *Phonogram*: a monthly magazine devoted to the science of sound and recording of speech. 1891-1893. New York. Monthly. "Official organ of the phonograph companies of the United States."

DLC: complete [TS 2301.P3A27]
NN: Microfilm: v. 1-2, no. 4/5, 8/9; 1891-Apr./May, Aug./Sept.
1892. [GRD: *ZAN-16]
44. *The Phonograph*: a musical news weekly. 1916-1978. New York.
Weekly. Title varies: July 2, 1919-Sept. 5, 1928, Phonograph and
talking machine weekly; Sept. 12, 1928-Dec. 6, 1933, Talking
machine and radio weekly; Dec. 13, 1933-Apr. 26, 1939, Radio
weekly; May 3, 1939-date, Radio and television weekly. Includes
mainly news of the recording industry.
DLC: v. 9-64. [TS2301.P3A4]
NN: v. 1, Apr. 1916-v. 122, Mar. 1978. (incomplete since July 5,
1965) [PRH: On microfilm in: *ZAN-*MP 68]
ONCG [Music Division]: v. 8, nos. 14, 15, 18, 21, 22, 15, 1919.
45. *The Phonograph Monthly Review*. See: *Music Lovers' Phonograph
Monthly Review*.
46. *Phonographische Zeitschrift*: Fachblatt für die gesamte Musik-
und Sprechmaschinen-Industrie. 1900-1938. Berlin, Germany.
Frequency varies. Organ of Internationaler Verein für Phono-
graphisches   Wissen,   Reichsverband   des   Deutschen
Sprechmaschinen-und Schallplatten-Handels, and others. Title
varies: Oct. 1933-1935, *Phonographische und Radio-Zeitschrift*;
1936-Mar. 1938, *Phonographische, Radio und Musikinstrumen-
ten Zeitschrift*. Absorbed Sept. 23, 1933: *Radio; Zeitschrift für das
Gesamte Radiowesen*. Absorbed July 27, 1938 by: *Der
Radiohandler*. Includes illustrated technical articles, industry
news, articles dealing with various uses for the phonograph.
DLC: Holdings not reported. [TK6540.R585]
NN: Jahrg. 1, Nr. 1, Aug. 15, 1900-Jahrg. 38, Nr. 6, Mar. 15, 1938.
(incomplete) [PRH: On microfilm in: *ZAN-*MP 9]
Staatsbibliothek Preussischer Kulturbesitz, Berlin: 1900-1938.
Lacking volumes 5, 22, 28, 33 [4 Op 29 888]
47. *The Phonoscope*: a monthly journal devoted to scientific and
amusement inventions appertaining to sound & sight. Nov.
1896-June 1900. New York. Monthly. Phonoscope Pub. Co.
Includes finely illustrated articles on talking machines, inventors,
artists etc. (example: Sarah Bernhardt listening to the Bettini
Micro-phonograph). Also, mention of a variety of artists such as:
Yvette Guilbert, Mr. Farko, Sarah Bernhardt, Melba, Mark
Twain, Lillie Langtry, M. Coquelin, Pol Plancon, Mme. Saville,
Lola Beeth, Ellen Terry, Julia Nelson & Olga Nethersole and their
cylinder recordings. Includes articles on the autograph, zerograph,
radiophone, megaphone and cathoscope; x-rays; automatic slot
machines; "picture projecting devices" such as: vitascope, phanto-
scope, eidoloscope, biograph, cinematographe, theatrograph &

kineopticon. Contains small reviews of films for "screen machines." Also includes listings of new records with artist & company; no record numbers. Listings of the latest popular songs and successes are given as well as listings of new films for projecting devices. There is a directory of exhibitors. There are articles for collectors on how to keep their recordings in good condition. There are notes from correspondents in London, Paris, Berlin, Amsterdam, Madrid, Alexandria, Constantinople, Australia, South America, Central America and Canada.
NN: v. 1, no. 1, Nov. 15, 1896–v. 4, June 1900. [Annex: 3-PFG +]

48. *Pishushchiĭ Amur*: zhurnal torgovykh izvestiĭ obshchestva "Grammofon." [Amur Company news] 1914–1916. Petrograd, Russia. Includes copious illustrations of early Russian grammophone factories and their various operational activities, illustrated articles of popular artists, listings of new recordings with artists and company label numbers, articles dealing with various uses of the gramophone such as: "The grammophone in the monastery."
CtY: no. 1–13; 1914–1916. [HSR]
Gosudarstvennaĭa Ordena Lenina Biblioteka SSSR imeni V. I. Lenina. [Lenin State Public Library] Moscow, USSR: Nos. 1–2, 1914; Nos. 3–9, 1915; Nos. 10–13, 1916.
Gosudarstvennaĭa Ordena Trudovogo Krasnogo Znameni Publichnaĭa Biblioteka imeni M. E. Saltykova-Shchedrina. [M. E. Saltykov-Shchedrin State Public Library] Leningrad, USSR: Nos. 1–2, 1914; Nos. 3–9, 1915; Nos. 10–13, 1916.

49. *Pishushchiĭ Amur I Grammofonnye Novosti*. 1910–1911. Moscow, Russia. Formerly: *Ofitsial'nye Izvestiĭa Aktsionernogo Obshchestva 'Grammofon.'*
Gosudarstvennaĭa Ordena Lenina Biblioteka SSSR imeni V. I. Lenina. [Lenin State Public Library] Moscow, USSR: Dec. 1910; Feb.–Apr. 1911.
Gosudarstvennaĭa Ordena Trudovogo Krasnogo Znameni Publichnaĭa Biblioteka imeni M. E. Saltykova-Shchedrina. [M. E. Saltykov-Shchedrin State Public Library] Leningrad, USSR: Dec. 1910; Feb., Apr. 1911.

50. *Power. RCA Victor Service Notes*. 1923–1945? Camden, New Jersey. Irregular. RCA Victor Company Inc.
British Library. National Sound Archive. 1923–1934.
NN: 1923–1945. (incomplete) [Annex: TTFA]
Vancouver Public Library. Vancouver, British Columbia. v. 63, 1926+.

51. *Radio Matériel*. 1925–? Paris, France. Monthly. Title changed to: *Radio et Phono Matériel*: revue mensuelle des négociants en T.S.F. et machines parlantes.

Bibliothèque Nationale, Département de la Phonothèque
Nationale et de L'Audiovisuel. Paris, France: No. 1, 1925- [B.N.
Imprimés Jo 62 808 (incomplete holding)]

52. *Radio Merchant.* 1905-1934? New York. Monthly. Other titles:
Talking Machine World, etc.
NN: v. 1, Jan. 15, 1905-Dec. 1928; 1929-1934 (Talking machine
world etc.) [Annex: 3-TTFA+]

53. *Record Review.* 1920?-1921? New York. bimonthly. Columbia
Graphophone Co., Educational Department.
NN: Sept./Oct. 1920, Jan./Feb. 1921. [PRH: *L (Sample file)]

54. *Revue des Machines Parlantes.* 1919-1929. Paris, France.
Monthly. Title changed to *Machines Parlantes et Radio*, with no.
120, Oct. 1929. Edité par L'Office général de la Musique.
Bibliothèque Nationale, Département de la Phonothèque
Nationale et de L'Audiovisuel. Paris, France: No. 1, 1919?-no. 236,
août 1939. Since no. 99, février 1929, but incomplete. [B.N. Imprimés Jo 63 247] 1930 -[B.N. Phonothèque Per 192] Since no. 117,
1929 -[Bibliothèque du Conservatoire Bp 181]

55. *Revista Fonografica Italiana*; periodico mensile illustrato. 1900-?
Milan, Italy, Monthly.
CtY: N. 13-24, 1900-? [HSR]

56. *Sound Wave*; the gramophone journal. 1906-1941. Finsbury,
England. Monthly. Title varies: v. 1, no. 3,-v. 22. 1906-1917, *The
Sound Wave and Talking Machine Record*. Incorporates: *The
Phono Trader & Recorder*. Includes articles on popular artists,
listings of recordings from various record companies such as
Gramophone, Genuine Edison, Sterling, Columbia, Odeon,
Zonophone, White, Beka, Neophone, Imperial, Edison Bell, giving
label nos., composers and artists, large section of record reviews,
technical articles dealing with fine points of recording and play-
back, articles dealing with novel uses for the phonograph, such as
street gospel meetings, the improvment of Jewish synagogue cha-
zan singers etc.
NN: v. 1, no. 1, Nov. 1906-v. 22, May 1928. (incomplete) [PRH:
*LA (Sound wave)]

57. *Die Sprechmaschine.* Fachzeitschrift für die gesamte
Sprechmaschinen-Industrie des In-und Auslandes. 1905-1914.
Berlin, Germany. Fortnightly.
Staatsbibliothek Preussischer Kulturbesitz. Berlin. v. 1, 1905-v.
10, 1914. [4 OS 3666]

58. *Die Stimme Seines Herrn.* 1910-1916. Berlin, Germany. Monthly.
Includes record listings with label nos., illustrated historical articles, illustrated articles on popular performers, record reviews.

NN: v. 1, Jan. 1910–v.8, Jan 1916. (incomplete) [PRH: on microfilm in *ZAN-*MP 37]
59. *Svet I Zvuk* [Light and sound]. 1905–1906. Saint Petersburg, Russia. Monthly. Includes illustrated technical articles, historical grammophone articles, lyrics of popular arias, current happenings in the grammophone industry. Formerly: *Grammofon I Fonograf.* CtY: 1905–1906. [HSR]
60. *The Talking Machine Journal*; the national journal of the talking machine industry. 1916–1957. New York. Monthly. Henderson [etc.]. Title varies: v. 26–31, 1929–Sept. 1931, *The Talking Machine and Radio Journal*; v. 31, no. 4–v. 46, no. 4, Oct. 1931–Apr. 1939, *Radio & Electric Appliance Journal*; v. 46, no. 5–v. 48, no. 16, May–Dec. 1939, *Radio-Television Journal*; v. 49–53, no. 3, v. 54, no. 8–v. 55, no. 2, 1940–Mar. 1942, Feb.–Aug. 1943, *Radio-Television Journal & the Talking Machine World*; v. 53, no. 4–v. 54, no. 7, Apr. 1942–Jan. 1943, *Radio Journal*; v. 55, no. 3–v. 63, no. 2, Sept. 1943–Aug. 1946, *Radio Television Journal* combining *Electric Appliance Journal* (slight variations); v. 63, no. 3–v. 66, no. 1, Sept. 1946–Jan. 1949, *Radio and Appliance Journal* (at head of title: *RAJ*); v. 66, no. 2–v. 73, no. 9, Feb. 1949–Sept. 1956, *Radio and Television Journal* (at head of title: *RTJ*). Vol. 47, no. 2–v. 48, no. 1, v. 61–62 omitted from numbering. Issues for May 1919–June 1923 include listing of "latest record releases." Includes industry news, record statistics (example: "The fastest selling Victor records"), historical articles.
DLC: v. 1–15?; v. 16–31. [TK6540.R26]
NN: v. 1, no. 3–v. 73, no. 9; Jan. 1917–Sept. 1956 (incomplete). [PRH: On microfilm in *ZAN-*MP 51]
61. *The Talking Machine News*. 1903–? London, England. Monthly and semimonthly. "The recognised organ of the trade." Includes illustrated articles on popular artists, historical articles, record reviews, technical articles dealing with the upkeep and proper use of talking machines and recordings, trade articles.
DLC: Complete. Details not provided.
NN: V. 3–4, no. 33–50, Jan.–Dec. 15, 1906. [PRH: *LA (Talking machine news)]
62. *The Talking Machine News and Journal of Amusements*. 1908?–? London, England. Monthly. Supersedes: *The Talking Machine News*. Consecutive numbers are odd-numbered only. Includes illustrated articles on popular artists, record reviews, musical articles, a column written by Mikhail Mordkin entitled: "The art of dancing and the talking machine," illustrated technical articles.
NN: V. 5 (new ser.), no. 157–177, Jan.–Nov. 1913. [PRH: *LA (Talking machine news and journal of amusements)]

63. *The Talking Machine World.* 1905-1934. New York. Title changed in Jan. 1929-July 1930 to: *Talking Machine World & Radio-Music*; in Aug. 1930, title changed to *Radio-Music Merchant*. In 1934, publication was absorbed by: *Radio & Electric Appliance Journal.* NN: v. 1-26, no. 7, Jan. 15, 1905-July 1930. STC: 3-TTFA+ (Radio merchant). Microfilm (negative): *ZZAN-2164]

64. *The Tonearm.* 1917?-1919? Bridgeport, Conn. Monthly. Columbia Phonograph Co. Inc., American Graphophone Co., Columbia Graphophone Manufacturing Co.
    NN: 1917-1918? [STC: TNK]

65. *The Total Eclipse.* 1920?-? U.S.A. Monthly. "Published monthly by the Eclipse Musical Company in the interests of Victor merchants."
    ONCG [Music Division]: Mar., Apr., May/June 1920.

66. *Victor Educational Bulletin.* 1916-1918.
    ONCG [Music Division]: No. 1, Dec. 30, 1916-no. 29, June 1918; nos. 30 & 32 (undated). (nearly complete)

67. *The Victor Tourist.* 1919?-? For the Victor traveling staff.
    ONCG [Music Division]: Aug. 1919.

68. *The Voice*; the magazine of the Gramophone Company Ltd. 1916-? Hayes, Middlesex, England. Irregular.
    CtY: v. 3, no. 7, 1919? [HSR]
    NN: v. 26-v. 35, 1942-1954 (incomplete). [PRH: *LA (Voice)]
    ONCG [Music Division]: v. 8, nos. 1, 6, 8-11, 1924; v. 9, nos. 1-2, 8, 10, 11, 1925; v. 10, nos. 1, 3, 4, 6/7, 9, 10, 1926; v. 11, nos. 5-9, 11, 12, 1927; v. 12, nos. 3, 5, 6, 10, 12, 1928; v. 13, nos. 1, 2, 4-9, 1929; v. 14, nos. 1-8, 10, 1930.

69. *The Voice of the Victor*; the trade journal of the Victor Talking Machine Co. 1906-1930? Camden, New Jersey. Monthly. Includes industry news, articles dealing with different uses for the gramophone, listings of new recordings with label nos., artists, composers, reviews.
    CSt: v. 1, no. 2-v. 15, no. 3, May 1906-Mar. 1920 (incomplete) (Microfilm copy of holdings in New York Public Library).
    NN: v. 1, no. 2-v. 15, no. 3, May 1906-Mar. 1920 (incomplete) [PRH: *LA Victor Talking Machine Company. The Voice of the Victor)]
    ONCG [Music Division]: v. 8, nos. 5, 7, 8, 1913; v. 9, nos. 8-10, 1914; v. 10, nos. 4, 6, 8-12, 1915; v. 11, no holdings, 1916; v. 12, nos. 1-12, 1917; v. 13, nos. 1-5, 7-12, 1918; v. 14, nos 5-12, 1919; v. 15, no. 1, 1920; v. 16, no. 9, 1921; v. 17, nos 5, 10, 12, 1922; v. 18, nos. 1, 2, 8, 1924; v. 20, no. 3, 1925; v. 21, nos. 1, 4, 5, 1926; v. 22, nos. 1, 2, 5 (June/July), 6, (Aug.), 8 (Sept.) 1927; v. [23], nos. [3], 5, 7

(July/Aug.), 8(Autumn), 9(Dec.), 1928; v. 24, no. 1, 1929; v. 24, no. 6 (late fall), 1930.

70. *Vsemirnoe Tekhnicheskoe Obozrenie*: ezhemes͡iảchnyĭ politekhnicheskiĭ zhurnal. 1898–1917. Saint Petersburg, Russia. Monthly. Publichna͡ia Biblioteka imeni M. E. Saltykova-Shchedrina. [M. E. Saltykov-Shchedrin State Public Library] Leningrad, USSR: Nos. 1–3, 1898; Nos. 4–12, 1–3, 1899; Nos. 4–12, 1900; 1900/1901–1907/ 1908 (24 numbers annually); 1908/1909–1915/1916 (12 numbers annually); Nos. 1–3, 1916.

71. *Weekly Bulletin*. [Victor] 1919?–? ONCG [Music Division]: no. 11, Mar. 21, 1919–no. 45, Nov. 22, 1919 (incomplete).

ADDENDA

New publications not already in the bibliography.

72. *Elektrische Nachrichtentechnik.* 1924–1943? Berlin, Germany, Monthly? Publisher: K. W. Wagner.
NN: 1924–? [STC]
Phonogrammarchiv der Oesterrichischen Akademie der Wissenschaften, Vienna: vol. 4, Jan. 1927–vol. 20, 1943.

73. *Grammotechnik.* 1929?–1932? Prague, Czechoslovakia. Verband für Industrie und Handel der Grammophon- und Musikinstrumenten-Branche in der CSSR, Prag.
Phonogrammarchiv der Oesterrichischen Akademie der Wissenschaften, Vienna: vol. 1, no. 2, Dec. 1929–vol. 4/9–10, Dec. 1932.

74. *Die Tonwiedergabe.* 1929?–1938? Vienna, Austria. Fachblatt für Industrie, Handel und Export aller an der Tonwiedergabe interessierten Kreise.
NN: v. 9, nos. 3–12, 1936; v. 10, nos. 2, 4–8, 1937; v. 11, nos. 1–8, 1938.
[Annex: 3-TTFA]
Phonogrammarchiv der Oesterrichischen Akademie der Wissenschaften, Vienna: v. 2, Feb. 1929–v. 11, 1938.

75. *Unterricht und Sprechmaschine.* 1908?–1914? Stuttgart, Germany. Publisher: Wilhelm Violet.
Phonogrammarchiv der Oesterrichischen Akademie der Wissenschaften, Vienna: v. 4, no. 1, Feb. 1912–v. 6, no. 6, Dec. 1914.

REFERENCE SOURCES

Dictionary catalog of the Research Libraries of The New York Public Library, 1911-1971. New York: The New York Public Library: printed & distributed by G. K. Hall & Company, 1979.

Gisondi, Gary-Gabriel. Sound recordings periodicals: a preliminary union catalog of pre-LP-related holdings in member libraries of the Associated Audio Archives. *ARSC (Association for Recorded Sound Collections) Journal*, v. X, no. 1, 1978, p. 37-65.

McCallum, David Ian. "Collecting in Australia," *Hillandale*. No. 166, Feb.1989, p. 162-163.

Mott, Frank Luther. *A History of American Magazines 1885-1905*. Cambridge, Mass.: Harvard University Press, 1957.

New York Times Index. 1889-1890. New York: The New York Times Company, 1966.

Poole, Mary & William I. Fletcher. *Poole's Index to Periodical Literature*. 45h & 5th supplements: Jan. 1, 1897-Jan. 1, 1902; Jan. 1, 1902-Jan. 1, 1907. Gloucester, Mass.: Peter Smith, 1963.

Read, Oliver & Walter L. Welch. *From Tin Foil to Stereo*. Indiana: Howard W. Sams & Co., 1977.

Reader's guide to periodical literature. v. 1, 1900-1904. Minneapolis: H. W. Wilson Company, 1905.

Revista hispanoamericanas. Indice bibliografico 1843-1935. Recopilado por Sturgis E. Leavitt. Santiago de Chile: Jose Toribio Medina, 1960.

Rodgers & Hammerstein Archives of Recorded Sound, The New York Public Library. Periodicals shelf list.

The Subject Index to Periodicals. Issued at the request of the Library Association. 1915-1916, 1917/19. London, The Library Association, 1916-.

Willing's British and Irish press guide. v. 19, 1892. London, England. (Variant title: *Willing's press guide*.)

Zeitschriften-Datenbank. Germany.

THE NEW YORK REVIEW

by Maryann Chach

The *New York Review* had its genesis in the great theatrical wars between Klaw and Erlanger, and the Shuberts at the turn of the century. Marc Klaw and Abraham Lincoln Erlanger controlled the Theatrical Syndicate, the most powerful theatre operation in the country. A trust of theatrical producers and theatre owners, the Syndicate controlled most of the hit plays and musicals on the New York stage. This control of "product" gave Klaw and Erlanger leverage in negotiating favorable bookings with independent theatre owners across the country. Theatre owners who did not ally themselves with the Syndicate and agree to its terms often found themselves without a booking or unable to book the productions their audiences wanted to see. At the same time a producer who did not like the Syndicate's terms might find himself unable to book a profitable tour, forced to play secondary houses or make large geographical jumps between tour stops. Through the Syndicate, Klaw and Erlanger owned, operated or influenced many of the major theatres in the country. The Shubert Brothers challenged the Syndicate and eventually reversed the balance of power. In a few short years they became the dominant force in the American theatre and remained in that position throughout their lives.

The Shubert Brothers – Sam, Lee and J.J. – grew up in Syracuse, New York. As a boy, Sam got his first theatrical job acting in a touring company of David Belasco's *May Blossoms* that played Syracuse. Sam retired from the stage to the behind-the-scenes activities of the box office – selling tickets, bookkeeping and,

---

MARYANN CHACH is the Archivist of the Shubert Archive. She has an M.A. in Cinema Studies from New York University and an M.L.S. from Columbia University.

eventually, managing theatres. He brought his two brothers, Lee and J.J. into the business and they gradually acquired several theatres upstate. With their business acumen, the Shuberts assembled financial backing from a number of investors and were ready to challenge Broadway.

When Sam and Lee Shubert arrived in New York City in 1900 (J.J. stayed in Syracuse to manage their upstate holdings), they tried to do business with the Syndicate but often found themselves, like many others, treated in a highhanded fashion – having bookings abruptly cancelled, etc. The Shuberts took on the Syndicate by advocating an "Open Door" policy which meant that they wanted the freedom to do business with whomever they liked. This put the Shuberts at war with the Syndicate.

The next salvo was fired by the daily theatrical and sporting newspaper, the *Morning Telegraph*. According to Lee Shubert, "nasty little digs at Sam or J.J. or me began to appear in the *Telegraph*" and Lee felt that the reporter, critic and columnist Rennold Wolf was responsible for the unsigned comments. Sam Shubert had hired Wolf to do some press work for the Shuberts in publications other than the *Telegraph*. Apparently Wolf was also working for the Syndicate and the Syndicate paid him better than the Shuberts. The *Telegraph* became closely allied with Klaw and Erlanger, boosting their shows, while vilifying the Shuberts who finally withdrew their advertising. Lee described a meeting with the *Telegraph's* editor Bill Lewis which was meant to smooth over past differences. Lee asked Lewis to stop the *Telegraph's* unjust attacks on the Shuberts and Lewis responded that the editorial policy of the *Telegraph* could not be controlled by threats of withdrawing advertising. Lee accused Rennold Wolf of being on the Syndicate's payroll and said the Syndicate controlled the *Telegraph's* policy. This break led to the Shuberts looking for a medium to express their policy and views and to defend themselves against the Syndicate.

The first issue of *The New York Review*, the weekly trade paper that the Shuberts created in response to the *Telegraph* and the Syndicate, appeared on August 29, 1909. It was issued on Sundays in three, sometimes four, sections (a pictorial section, one or two news sections and a magazine; each section separately paged). Milton Wolf, who was married to the Shuberts' sister Dora and managed the clothing store Joseph's, was listed as President and Emmanuel M. Klein was Secretary and Treasury. They seem to have been figureheads and had as little do with the actual running of the newspaper as possible. Sam Weller, the editor, and Charles Daniel, business and advertising manager, actually ran the paper with the persistent help of their not-so-silent partners, the Shuberts.

From the beginning it was obvious that Lee and J.J. Shubert controlled the *Review*, although neither of their names was listed on the paper's masthead. For one thing, there is no correspondence between Milton Wolf and Weller, Daniel, or either of the Shuberts regarding the *New York Review*. There is, however, abundant correspondence between the Shubert Brothers and Weller and Daniel. For instance, in an effort to boost the advertising base and put the newspaper into the black, Daniel enlisted the help of an advertising man, Sigmund Klee of Ward and Gow, who wrote letters to clients on the *Review's* behalf. In a letter dated October 5, 1910, Klee wrote: "My friend, Lee Shubert, of the Shubert Theatrical Company, controls the New York Review, a weekly paper with illustrated supplements devoted largely to theatrical and sporting news . . ." Lee's response to Daniel's initiative was: "I note in Mr. Klee's letter to Mr. Sandlass that he mentions the fact that I control the New York Review. Hereafter please do not make this statement. I simply want you to say that I am interested in this publication."

Lee also wrote letters to the managers of Shubert houses and independent houses urging them and their staff to subscribe and support the *Review*. Lee and J.J. both helped with procuring advertisements for the newspaper on a quid pro quo basis. Frequent advertisers in the *Review* were often accorded free tickets to a show. Some advertisers expected something more substantial. I. Miller advertised and got orders for shoes from the Shuberts. Cammeyer, the shoemaker, was reluctant to continue advertising because "your promise . . . that theatrical business from the firm of Shubert would be very shortly forthcoming" had not been kept. Eventually, Cammeyer received some Shubert business. Ditto Max & Mahieu, costumers: "We know very well that you rather would like to see our Ad enlargened [sic] but for an argument we call your attention to one fact, in the last program of the Wintergarden, you find for instance, Paquin, Callot & Worth, Paris; . . . Hugo Baruch & Co., Berlin; Miller, New York . . . We couldn't find any ad of them in The Review."

Other advertisers expected to see the name of their product or store advertised on drop curtains or displayed prominently in productions. Daniel to J.J. Shubert (October 17, 1911):

> "The New England Button Shoe manufacturers are pressing me for something definite in regard to the button shoe number at the Winter Garden.

They have asked for a conference in the matter on Wednesday afternoon at which time they are prepared to execute formal contract for the $2,000 in advertising provided you have song and dance number in satisfactory shape."

Gimbel Bros. paid for an ad in the *Review* in exchange for a drop curtain in the new Winter Garden Show. Daniel had to stall the advertising director at Gimbels while he pleaded with Lee to let him know if the drop curtain would go into the show and asked Lee "not [to] refer this to Mr. J.J. as he gets mad at me every time I mention these drop curtains."

Several automobile companies, including the White Automobile Company, promised advertising to the *Review* if Mr. Lee or Mr. J.J. would consider purchasing an automobile and recommending their product to friends. [NB: in 1912, an automobile could cost anywhere from $2000 to $8000.] In at least one issue, the *Review* ran a pictorial spread of stage stars in their automobiles and the captions included the name of the automobile manufacturers. Joseph's, Milton Wolf's company, advertised in the *Review* but Charles Daniel, the business manager, had much difficulty collecting payment; he wrote many tactfully worded letters to Lee and J.J. to enlist their help in settling the bills. Another type of advertising was the theatre giveaways and companies that gave away samples of their products to the theatre audiences including Lindt chocolate, Djer-Kiss perfume and Ex-Lax. One advertising tie-in that the Shubert Archive can document clearly is a "City Girl" number in a Winter Garden revue (probably, the *Passing Show of 1916*). J.J. to Daniel [May 11, 1916]:

We are getting out the following dresses for the girls in new show: –
San Francisco, orange girl.
Los Angeles, film girl.
Detroit, automobile . . .
Philadelphia, quaker girl.
Pittsburg[h], iron and steel . . .
Milwaukee, blue ribbon beer girl.
We can change these to suit the cigarette girls or blue ribbon beer, automobile of some kind made in Detroit, and for railroads Phoebe Snow girl, so please see Mr. Simmons as quickly as possible and he will give you full information.

Daniel to J.J. Shubert [May 20, 1916]:

The Lackawanna Railroad wants the Phoebe Snow Girl in the number at the Winter Garden to represent Buffalo . . . I think the Detroit Cadillac Automobile Co. will take the one representing Detroit . . .

At first, it was hoped that once its subscribers and advertisers had placed the *Review* on a firm financial footing, the newspaper might eventually become a daily or, at least, semi-weekly, but that never happened. It remained a weekly for its entire 22 year run. If the initial impetus behind the *Review* was to combat the Syndicate and all it stood for, then it certainly achieved its goal in the early issues. Nearly every news section featured a barbed anti-Syndicate cartoon by Howell. Many of these are extremely inventive and satirize Abe Erlanger who is portrayed in a baseball suit, swinging a bat and wearing a Napoleonic hat. Others illustrate the power behind the *Morning Telegraph*: Ringmaster Erlanger forcing Bill Lewis, the editor of the *Telegraph*, and Rennold Wolf to jump through hoops. Some border on the malicious – Erlanger's head on the body of a rat. Howell also did more flattering caricatures of performers. Shubert shows, the shows of their allies, and performers in those shows were, of course, featured in articles and photographs in the *Review*. Articles about the latest Syndicate outrage or any scandal touching them often made the front page of the news section. One of the articles settled the score with Rennold Wolf. Wolf's wife Hope Booth was destitute in Italy and the *Review* headline read "Hope Booth, ill and penniless in Italy, will be given benefit at Casino next Sunday under auspices of the Review."

The majority of articles were not signed which may indicate that they were press releases which the *Review* simply reprinted without editing. Many of the pieces were orchestrated by the Shubert Bros. Lee Shubert to Charles Daniel [July 16, 1916]: "In the future when you have a front page, ask me what to use. Do not use people like Alice Brady who don't do us a bit of good. Use only people who are working for us." In a letter to J.J. Shubert [November 6, 1911], Colgate Baker, interviewer and journalist for the *Review*, wanted to do a story which would hint at the real reason for Fannie Ward's law suit against Marc Klaw for violating her contract: Klaw was angry at Ward for discarding him for another lover. Memos suggest the J.J. and Lee discussed whether or not to publish the Fannie Ward story but there are no surviving *Reviews* for that period which would give us the outcome. In the mid-teens, the *Review* began to cover the moving pictures extensively and even devoted a section to the movies. At around this time, the Shuberts were investing in World Films. Sporting news was included in the *Review* but never to the extent that the theatre was featured.

The cast of the *New York Review* each brought a certain flair to the paper. Samuel MacLeary Weller led a colorful life before settling down with the paper. He was born in Columbus, Texas, around 1876 and joined Teddy Roosevelt's Rough Riders in the Spanish American War. As a journalist on the New York *Telegraph*, he recounted the exploits of the Rough Riders based on his own experiences. Later he covered stories in Canarsie, Brooklyn, for the New York *Journal* and sent his copy via carrier pigeon back to the office. Weller remained with the *Review* until its end in 1931 after which he worked as a publicist for the Lunts, Maurice Evans, Walter Huston, and Walter Hampden. Weller often wrote the lead anti-Syndicate article in the *Review* news section. Little is known about the personal or professional life of business and advertising manager Charles Daniel. From his everyday memos, one can see that he was a stickler for details and somewhat ingenious in coming up with advertising tie-ins and in hounding advertisers with unpaid bills. Daniel left the *Review* in 1926 for a job with a Wall Street firm. The interviewer Colgate Baker was born in Kobe, Japan around 1872. His father was a tea merchant and his mother, an Episcopalian missionary. He attended Phillips Andover Academy, and then studied at Yale for a year before entering West Point. Ill health forced him to withdraw from West Point but he later joined the regular army and fought Indians in the West. All this, no doubt, priming him for his battles against the Syndicate and with the Shuberts. Baker was married to actress/soprano Freda Gallick whose career he never failed to boost to the Shuberts. Baker to Lee Shubert [August 9, 1911]: "If Miss Fay Templeton does not accept your offer to her to play Little Buttercup in 'Pinafore,' I respectfully suggest that you consider Mrs. Baker for the role. She has made a great success in eccentric characters and I know she would be an ideal Buttercup, she acts better than she sings, and you know what she can do vocally."

The *Review* ran from 1909 until sometime in 1931. (*The Union List of Serials* suggests it ceased publication in 1937 but several sources in the Shubert Archive put the *Review*'s demise in 1931). The Archive has an almost pristine bound copy of the first year and a half of the *Review* (August 29, 1909 to February 18, 1911). Because the bound volumes are newsprint and in fragile condition, they have been microfilmed and researchers are required to use the microfilm. The only other source for the New York *Review* is the Billy Rose Theatre Collection, PARC, The New York Public Library. That collection has 6 reels of microfilm covering the dates 1909 to 1919 (For volumes 1 and 6 through 19, approximately half of each volume is extant) and only the microfilm record survives. The Archive hopes to find the missing volumes someday.

All quotations from correspondence are from sources at the Shubert Archive. The Archive is open for research by scholars by appointment only. Please contact Maryann Chach, Archivist, Shubert Archive, Lyceum Theatre, 149 West 45th Street, New York, NY 10036.

692   La Petite Adelaide

an American, named Hughes. In former days, Adelaide danced solo, or with no more company than her own double reflection in a pair of mirrors, in a pretty conceit called "The Three Graces." Now she has all her own graces, plus the effective support of Hughes; and the pair "write their own stuff," as the stage folk say, giving a very acceptable imitation of the prevailing European *ballet d'action,* or descriptive story-dancing, in which physical "lines," curves, and rhythmic movements supply the place of words in opera.

"My ideal is Pavlowa," says Adelaide, "and I am ambitious to do nothing but descriptive dances, as she does. But there is not yet a demand here for nothing but artistic things, so we have to be careful, and hold back some of our best bits, the true dance art of the future, for the present."

Adelaide's most convincing eloquence is in her quick, graceful, and sinuous movements, which actually seem to give utterance to the accompanying music, rather than to have their pace set by it. Technically, her training has been American from the start, and that fact

"I don't know what my feet will be, but I guess is still quite some ways ahead

accounts for the zest with which presumably blasé European have viewed her performance.

"I remember, as a little to dancing on the sidewalks of Tro to the music of a hand-organ she tells us. "They sent me dancing-school early, a it was there the idea of goi on the stage was first put in my head. Mrs. Jacques Kru took me in hand at the beginning, and th I went on to Fransioli. It wasn't so mu talent that made a dancer of me, as was holding a pole above my head at arm length, and in this strained position cross the floor on the tips of my toes—practisi this sort of thing for months together, un I must either die from fatigue or else be al to do the pirouette. Then come the high kick the back bend, the split, the double twirl of t feet in the air, and a lot of other hand things— then you are only a step-dancer, with the ballet still learn." And as compared with the ballet, all the rest

Adelaide and Hughes in their "spe-

Adelaide and Hughes in their specialty ballroom number, "The Hoop Whirl," from *The Passing Show of 1912.* Billy Rose Theatre Collection, The New York Public Library.

The "No Clasp Dance" from *The Louisville [Kentucky] Herald*, April 14, 1912. Billy Rose Theatre Collection, The New York Public Library.

Joan Sawyer and John Jarrott in the "Congo Trot," 1914. Billy Rose Theatre Collection, the New York Public Library.

Vernon and Irene Castle in their One Step, as reported in *The Akron [Ohio] Press,* ca. 1912. Billy Rose Theatre Collection, The New York Public Library.

Maurice and [Florence] Walton as featured on a sheet music cover. Private Collection.

Advertisement for Victrolas by Norman Price, 1914. Picture Collection, The New York Public Library.

Advertisement for *Motion Picture Dancing Lessons* featuring Joan Sawyer and Wallace McCutcheon from the *Kalem Kalendar*, 1913. Billy Rose Theatre Collection, The New York Public Library.

THE DOLLY SISTERS IN "HIS BRIDAL NIGHT."

ka and Yancsi in one of their several picturesque Lucile costumes, dancing dow
the final curtain on the Lawrence Rising-Margaret Mayo farce at the Republic

The Dolly Sisters in *His Bridal Night*, 1916. Photograph by White Studios. Gowns by Lucile, Ltd. Billy Rose Theatre Collection, The New York Public Library.

Cover of the Reel Thirty-Three issue of *Our Mutual Girl Weekly,* featuring a photograph by Arnold Genthe of Norma Phillips, who starred (unbilled) as "Margaret." Billy Rose Theatre Collection, The New York Public Library.

GOWNS FOR MATINÉE, MUSICALE AND TEA
By Janet Claghorne
[Photograph by Joel Feder Exclusively for Our Mutual Girl Weekly]

BEAUTIFUL and ingenious are the new demi-toilettes for mid-winter occasions. Quaint, full skirted models and Russian effects lead. A new costume which, despite being developed in rich blacks, is essentially youthful and piquant, has a black velvet skirt bordered with skunk, flaring in deep ripples. The bodice is of black taffeta, flecked with velvet motifs à la Pierrot. The square-cut low neck is edged with skunk, and, in the back, an exceedingly high, flaring collar with spear-pointed corners also shows a jagged line of the fur.

Two black velvet ribbons, falling straight from the waist-line in the front, are tipped with red roses, and a red rose is caught at the lower left side of the high-waisted bodice. Long, tight sleeves are banded with skunk at the wrists, and a small, high turban of black velvet, fitting snugly in a "widow's peak" over the forehead, is tipped exactly at the crown of the head with a tail of the fur.

The striking gown here reproduced is exceptionally chic. It is of black satin-striped white chiffon and black chiffon velvet, and is distinguished by the long Russian tunic to which the striped chiffon lends itself so gracefully. The blouse is mainly white chiffon, with bolero effect of the stripe and a crossing of black velvet ribbons across the bust. The white chiffon collar is edged with pure white ermine, bands of which also outline the large armholes.

Yoke and underskirt are of the chiffon velvet, and the very artistic girdle is fashioned of white picot ribbon embroidered with heavy roses in pastel shades. A very large hat of black velvet, trimmed with black gourba, flecked with white, completes this most attractive costume.

A gown which was a cross between a Russian peasant's smock and a crusader's surcoat recently was seen at an exclusive afternoon function in New York. It was an engaging little frock of pearl grey chiffon cloth with underdress of white charmeuse, the chiffon overdress of which was embroidered in grey in a ring design

suggesting a coat of mail worn beneath.

The design appeared on the front of the bodice, running straight across the arms. It also decorated the fore-shortened tunic. A broad, loose band of kolinsky—the softest and duskiest trimming fur of the season—held in the fulness about the hips, and a narrow band of the fur encircled the white chiffon collar which rose in high flaring points.

Russian—though cast in the most ethereal materials and without the prevalent touch of fur—is a dainty afternoon receiving gown of pale pink, transparent black and fancy beading. Over a slim sheath of flesh-tinted satin clings a long smock-tunic of dull black tulle, without a suggestion of fulness in the slim bodice though flaring about the bottom.

The tulle overdress is perforated with tiny gold beads, and is weighted at neck and hem with a simply wrought design in black and gold beading. Through this trimming runs a tracery of turquoise, and the girdle, worn low and heavily tasselled, echoes the turquoise note. Filmy lace, against a pale pink satin petticoat, foams about the ankles. Stockings of flesh-tinted silk and rosettes, dull black satin slippers are worn.

The restaurant frock demands smartness and prettiness, but also a well-defined restraint. A certain New York shop, noted for the modish refinement of its original models, is showing such a frock developed in black satin, black Chantilly lace and black net. It has the new high ceinture which forms part of the bodice, and the slim satin underskirt is veiled in two deep tunics of the lace. The front and the long, close sleeves are of net, and a dainty box-plaited net ruche stands up at the back of the neck. A dinner gown of irreproachable taste, this frock for restaurant or hotel dining-room wear, still successfully avoids the intimate and more elaborate look of the dinner costume to be worn in private.

No. J. M.
Gidding & Co.

Bridge Gown of Black Satin-striped White Chiffon

[6] x]

Fashion page from the *Motion Picture Supplement*, November 1915.
Billy Rose Theatre Collection, The New York Public Library.

110

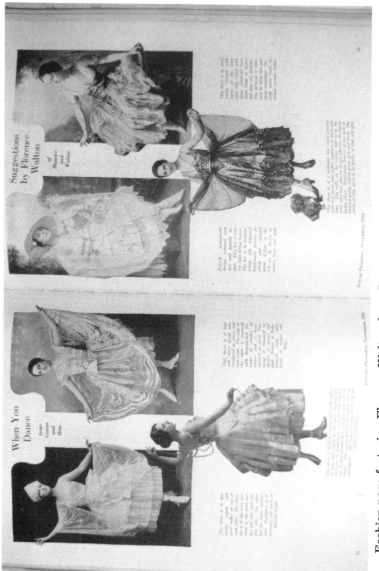

Fashion page featuring Florence Walton from *Picture Progress*, November 1916, pages 12-13. Billy Rose Theatre Collection, The New York Public Library.

111

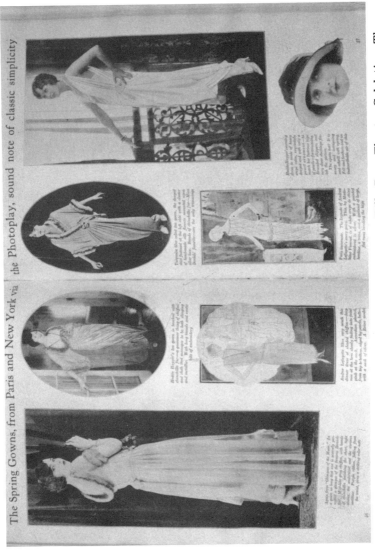

The Spring Gowns, from Paris and New York *via* the Photoplay, sound note of classic simplicity

Fashion page from *Photoplay*, April 1923, pages 46-47. Billy Rose Theatre Colelction, The New York Public Library.

112

Jane's New Gowns

Paul Grenbeaux

JANE NOVAK has always been the screen's most abused heroine. Fate's stepchild. She has been beaten and neglected—she has been forced to wear rags and tatters. A gingham frock and and mackinaw have been her party clothes. But now, in her latest picture, she is blossoming out in Paris gowns and coats. Her first chance to have a trousseaux!

ON the left—Jane in a wrap of beige caracul, created for her by the Boie Soeurs. The collar is made of Kolinsky. On the right she is seen in what has been called "Jane's gown of gold." It cost—whisper it—twenty-five hundred dollars! Gold lace, gold cloth, gold embroidery, gold tulle—and Miss Novak's gleaming golden hair!

Fashion page from *Photoplay,* March 1923. Billy Rose Theatre Collection, The New York Public Library.

Advertisement from *Photoplay,* March 1923. Billy Rose Theatre Collection, The New York Public Library.

Advertisement from *Photoplay,* March 1923. Billy Rose Theatre Collection, The New York Public Library.

RESEARCHING EXHIBITION BALLROOM DANCE: EXPLORING NON-TRADITIONAL SOURCES

by Julie Malnig

In recent years the United States has witnessed the resurgence of exhibition ballroom dance whose roots date back to the early 1900s. Following a hiatus of activity in the 1950s and '60s, professional ballroom dancers now appear before packed audiences. They perform on diverse stages, from Carnegie Hall to Roseland. Broadway extravaganzas, such as *Tango Argentino*, helped revive the Latin ballroom dances. And dance teachers report that enrollments in ballroom classes are on the rise. Despite the early popularity of exhibition ballroom dance and its current revival, there exist few published texts and scholarly articles on this topic. Therefore, in researching exhibition ballroom dance, it became necessary to ferret out a variety of non-traditional – and less readily accessible – sources. This article will explore how the dance and theatre researcher locates and uses these materials.

During the 1910s exhibition ballroom dance was one of the most popular forms of theatrical dance in the United States. In this dance form, male-female teams perform stylized, often flamboyant renditions of contemporary social dances. Social dances refer to those dances performed by the public for recreational enjoyment, while exhibition dances are those numbers performed by professionals for theatrical presentation. The exhibition teams rose to prominence as a result of their performances in vaudeville, the musical theatre, and the cabaret, where they transformed ordi-

JULIE MALNIG holds a Ph.D. in Performance Studies from New York University. The title of her dissertation is "Exhibition Ballroom Dance and Popular Entertainment." She currently teaches in the Gallatin Division of NYU and is an editor of *Women & Performance* journal.

nary social dances of the day, such as the Fox Trot and the One Step, into forms of theatrical art.

A unique facet of exhibition ballroom dance is its relationship to the social dances performed by the public. The teams invented many dances performed by the public and inspired them to dance, as well. In the cabaret, for example, the precursor of the night-club, exhibition teams typically performed a series of numbers, after which the public rushed to the dance floor to try out their own versions. In essence, the teams helped engender a national "dance craze." They advocated freer, less restrained forms of movement than those characteristic of 19th century ballroom dancing. The dancers also presented romantic images of women and men in public settings, which the public found appealing.

To understand the ballroom dance phenomenon, it was necessary to locate materials that would reveal why exhibition ballroom dancers had become so popular; what were the role of exhibition ballroom dancers in promoting dance among the public; and the nature of the dances themselves. One particular challenge was to determine, for example, the difference between an *exhibition* Turkey Trot – as performed by professionals – and one performed by the (amateur) dancing public.

As the dance/theatre historian researching the early 20th century knows, the majority of research materials are to be found not in books and journals, but rather in a variety of other published sources such as newspaper and magazine articles and reviews. The historian also must seek out scripts, contracts, musical scores, sketches, and photographs. In researching exhibition ballroom dance I drew almost exclusively on newspaper and magazine clippings, dance instruction manuals, and photographs, as well as a number of "hidden" and less orthodox sources tucked away inside sheet music covers and the pages of record company catalogues. Many of the newspaper articles, located in scrapbooks on the dancers, could be identified only by periodical, date, or scrapbook number and collection. Despite the frequent lack of authorship and incompleteness of many of the citations, these materials nonetheless provided an invaluable source of information on the careers of the teams, their dances, and on the ways in which they were promoted and popularized.

Unfortunately for the researcher, reviews of dance in vaudeville and musical theatre productions often contain vague, general descriptions, such as "pleasing," "beautifully executed," and "graceful." This language is frustrating because it does not explain how the dances were pleasing, beautifully executed, or graceful. Of course, reviews are helpful in reconstructing the ways in which the dance numbers were interpolated into the shows, but they offer few clues about the look and shape of the dances themselves. To obtain information about the style and shape of dances, the researcher turns to dance instruction manuals of the period — those written by dance teachers and/or by professional dance teams. These books are generally step-by-step descriptions of dances with diagrams and illustrations.

There exist a wealth of other kinds of "dance manuals" from this period however, not located in books. Many newspaper and magazine features on exhibition ballroom teams regularly included descriptions and illustrations of the teams' dance steps, often with advice on how to adapt these numbers for the amateur. Sheet music usually featured prominent dance teams on the front covers, often in a signature pose. And the inside covers often featured descriptions of the dance itself. *Modern Dances*, a booklet of sheet music published by Knickerbocker Music in 1914, provided step-by-step illustrations and foot patterns for several popular dances of the day, from the Tango to the Hesitation Waltz. Sources such as these help the researcher determine the look of the dance and how it may have been taught. They also reveal important information about the popularization of ballroom dance. Newspapers, magazines, and sheet music were affordable, mass-distributed means of communication, which found their way into homes across the country. For fifty cents — the average price for sheet music in 1914 — the reader could get an introductory dance lesson.

To cull these sources one needs to consult a variety of research collections. Some of the most valuable newspaper and magazine features are to be found in personality "clipping files" and scrapbooks. Many of these articles, however, exist in fragments only. One of the most aggravating experiences for the researcher is to find an exciting description of a dance, only to discover that the last two paragraphs of text or several illustrations have been torn away. In these cases, if the name and date of the clipping are present, one can consult the newspaper publisher (if they are still in existence) to obtain the entire article. Or, collections such as the Newspaper Annex of The New York Public Library may have the entire piece in print or on microfilm. Since news of the teams appeared so regularly during the years 1911–1916 (the height of the "dance craze") another useful method is to select one or two prominent newspapers of the period and scan the entertainment or society pages (sections in which stories on the dancers were most likely to appear) over a three-to-six month period.

The dancers' scrapbooks were the basis for determining other potential sources of information. For example, some of the manuscripts contained fragments of articles from early film company magazines, such as *Universal Weekly*. This discovery led me directly to the original magazines, several of which featured valuable photographs from the teams' instructional dance films. The other important periodicals were phonograph catalogues, such as those published by Victor and Columbia recording companies, which contained listings of popular dance music of the period.

As is the case with most of this research, one source invariably leads to another. I discovered that phonograph catalogues functioned as yet another type of dance manual. These catalogues featured dance descriptions as well as photographs of professional teams in various poses. Clearly, the ballroom dance phenomenon gave a big boost to the music industry. Record producers, for example, churned out hundreds of new, danceable melodies, and the packaging of their catalogues reflected their attempt to appeal to the new dancing public. In addition to printing dance descriptions and photographs in their catalogues, record publishers hired some of the most renowned ballroom dancers of the day, such as Irene and Vernon Castle, to endorse their dance recordings.

The key to understanding the ballroom dance phenomenon lay in piecing together a variety of disparate sources from different disciplines – dance, theatre, music, and film. The following research examples are drawn from the period 1909-1918 – the heyday of exhibition ballroom dance. This was a period of ballroom dance history in which the professional teams directly influenced the dancing preferences of the public, and these materials illuminate that relationship.

MAGAZINE FEATURES

Most general interest magazines of the period 1911-1916 featured major stories on exhibition ballroom dancers. Periodicals such as *Scribners, Harper's Weekly, Colliers*, and *American Mercury* tended to feature articles chronicling the rise of the ballroom dance craze and proferring theories about the widespread popularity of the dance teams. The women's and fashion magazines, such as *Vogue, Ladies' Home Journal*, and *Vanity Fair* contained personality-oriented stories focusing on the glamorous lives of the teams.

The women's and fashion periodicals frequently published feature articles with accompanying photographic spreads documenting actual dances. In 1912, for example, *Cosmopolitan* featured an article on the acrobatic ballroom team of Adelaide and Hughes. It contained several photographs of their renowned "Hoop Whirl" dance, an exhibition number they had popularized in the Shubert Brothers' musical revue *The Passing Show of 1912*. The *Cosmopolitan* photographs proved to be exceptionally valuable since few other production photographs could be located. Also, the dance itself was a significant one, because it represented a particular, stylized form of ballroom dance — the acrobatic/adagio mode. (see photographs).

Many of these illustrated dance pieces were designed as tools for readers to learn the latest dances. For example, in 1914 the *Ladies' Home Journal* published a feature on the Castles' latest dances entitled "New Dances for This Winter." The piece contained directions for several dances, including pictures of the Castles in accompanying poses. Vernon Castle describes the Castle Gavotte to his readers:

> "We commence by rocking forward, you on your right foot and I on my left, for two beats (first photograph); then we rock backward on the other foot for two beats (second photograph). After that we take three walking steps forward for three beats, and pause in the second photograph for the last and eighth beat — ready to commence the step again. If this is gone over carefully you will have no difficulty in grasping what the step is, and this is really the only step in the modern Gavotte."[1]

Of course, it is difficult to determine if readers actually performed these steps and routines themselves, but we can conclude that these magazine features did function as dance manuals for the general public and provided basic information concerning movements and postures characteristic of early 20th-century ballroom dance. We know for certain that these mass subscription magazines reached millions of readers across the country and were a critical vehicle for disseminating news of the teams and their dances.

NEWSPAPER ARTICLES

Newspapers, as well, were a primary source of information on exhibition ballroom teams. All the major New York City newspapers published stories on the dancers, including the *New York Times*, the *New York Evening Journal*, the *New York Evening Post*, and the *New York Tribune*. And outside of New York City, articles could be found in papers such as the *Buffalo (NY)*

Enquirer, the *Louisville Herald*, and the *San Francisco Call*. Usually the articles served as promotional devices to publicize a team's vaudeville or musical theatre engagement. Many of these pieces contained detailed descriptions of dances from their shows. During the touring production of the musical *The Whirl of Society* (1912), the *Louisville Herald* featured an article entitled "The Latest Dances and How to Dance Them" with instructions by the star team of the show Jose Collins and Martin Brown. The dancers explain their exhibition number – the "No Clasp" dance – and then offer suggestions as to how to modify it for recreational use. The dance required the female partner to lean back against a sash held by her partner while both of them waltzed. As Jose Collins tells her readers:

> "It's not easy as you will see if you try, but it's exceedingly pretty, and a beginner would not need to bend very far back from the waist, and her partner could hold the ends of the sash loose . . . that would make a pretty effect and would not be hard or require much skill in dancing."[2]

Of course, the authorship of some of these articles is often suspect; it is likely that many of them were arranged – and even penned – by managers or press agents. However, one can attempt to verify the authenticity of the dance by comparing it with descriptions of the same dance in newspaper reviews, production photographs, and dance manuals of the period, where possible. See illustrations, pp. 99–106.

Some of the most intriguing sources were syndicated newspaper articles on ballroom dance. These articles, owned by national news organizations, appeared in newspapers across the country and were thus read by millions of readers. Typically, these "how to" pieces contained some of the most detailed dance instructions. A particularly lively series of syndicated articles written by the Dolly Sisters appeared in the 1916 *Newark Star Eagle*. The Dolly Sisters were a single-sex exhibition ballroom team; the basis of their act – known as a tandem act – involved their twin identities. During the week of October 23, 1916, the team appeared in the touring production of the musical farce *His Bridal Night* at the Broad Street Theatre in Newark, New Jersey. Each day of that week an article appeared in which the twin stars described another dance in their repertoire – from the Dolly Waltz to the Minuet Rag. As with other instructional articles of this kind, the dances were described in terms the amateur could understand. What made this series of articles unique was its finely rendered illustrations and the addition of the Dolly Sisters "opinions" on such matters as ballroom etiquette and the value of dancing in modern life.

MUSIC-RELATED SOURCES

SHEET MUSIC

Sheet music from the 1910s proved to be an extremely valuable source of information on exhibition ballroom dances. The popularization of ragtime music spawned a host of so-called "rag dances," such as the Turkey Trot and Grizzly Bear, performed to rollicking, syncopated rhythms. In turn, music publishers capitalized on the rag dance craze, and to promote their musical compositions, they featured the names and photographs of dance stars on the covers of their sheet music. The music companies also began a practice no doubt welcomed by the public – they featured accompanying dance instructions and in some cases diagrams and illustrations on the inside and back covers.

Sheet music of this sort helps to reconstruct dances in many ways. The music itself enables the researcher to determine the appropriate tempo at which the numbers were performed, and the descriptions suggest how the dances were adapted for amateur use. Frequently the dance instructions were written by prominent dance teachers of the period who may have been particularly interested in describing dances that were truly danceable. Sheet music for the 1914 Toddle Dance published by Joseph W. Stern & Co., contained instructions by noted dance teacher Mr. G. Hepburn Wilson. The explanation consisted of three basic "Figures" (dance configurations) and specified how many steps should be performed to each bar of music. Wilson seemed optimistic that the Toddle would catch on with the public when he stated, "I feel confident that many figures will be developed and created by the dancers themselves as soon as the swing and rhythm of the Toddle becomes familiar to them."[3] As mentioned earlier, sheet music was inexpensive, and therefore served as an affordable dance manual for the public.

RECORD CATALOGUES

Another "hidden" source of ballroom dance information can be located in monthly catalogues published by the major record companies of the 1910s, such as Victor and Columbia. These catalogues furnished supplemental background on the recordings, including names and dates of musical compositions and composers. While the dance craze was at its peak, these catalogues contained pages of listings of most of the known social dances of the day (along with the names of the musical compositions that accompanied them). Supposedly these listings represented dances performed by the public at major clubs and cabarets around the country. They included the Lame Duck Waltz, the Grizzly Trot, the Castle Walk, the Valse Boston, and many more. The catalogues also offered directions concerning the speed and tempo at which the dances could be performed. As the November 1914 Columbia Records catalogue noted:

> "Practically any of the tangos may be used for dancing the Maxixe simply by playing the record at a slightly faster tempo than the regular speed used for the tango."[4]

The Maxixe was another popular ballroom dance of the day that combined steps from the Tango and the Two-Step. Information such as that quoted above offers the researcher a glimpse of how the public, playing their Victrola at home, may have actually danced the number.

The record company catalogues also featured photographs of popular exhibition ballroom dancers. In fact, a publicity "war" of sorts developed between rival dancers Joan Sawyer and Irene and Vernon Castle. Columbia Records hired Sawyer as "dance master" to oversee the production of their dance recordings, while Victor Records employed the Castles to endorse their label. During the 1914 season both publications ran advertisements for the dancers' cabaret and theatre engagements, and they both provided illustrations and descriptions of the dancers' latest creations. The photographs in these publications were valuable (for the 1910s dancing public and for the contemporary researcher) because they depict the dancers in *sequential* steps and poses from the numbers.

MOTION PICTURE MEMORABILIA

Several exhibition ballroom teams of the 1910s appeared in silent film shorts—either instructional dance films or what were known as "exhibition reels," consisting of three or four exhibition numbers. These films were approximately 15–20 minutes in duration and typically appeared as an item on a standard vaudeville bill. Unfortunately, few if any of these films have survived. In their absence, the researcher turns to reviews and photographs (if any) in newspapers and film trade magazines. But the most valuable sources of written and visual information about these films are found in film company magazines, also known as press books. The film companies published these magazines, which were designed primarily to promote their upcoming features. These movie magazines, some of which can be located in the Theatre Collection of The New York Public Library, contain high quality reproductions of scenes from the films, detailed explanations of the plot (if there was one), and descriptions of the dance numbers. For example, *Kalem Kalendar*, published by the silent film company Kalem Film Studios, featured a piece on the instructional dance short *Motion Picture Dancing Lessons* (1913). The film starred the highly popular team of Joan Sawyer and Wallace McCutcheon who, logically enough, portray dance teachers. The movie opened at a fashionable cabaret where a group of amateur dancers are interrupted periodically by Sawyer and McCutcheon who demonstrate the "correct" method of performing the numbers. In the second sequence the exhibition team is shown at their dance studio giving ballroom lessons. The concluding scene — considered novel at the time — showed McCutcheon's lower limbs in isolation as he demonstrated correct foot positioning. A note in the article explained that vaudeville managers, when showing the film, could have live musicians play accompanying music in time with the dances.

Clearly, the Kalem company promoted *Motion Picture Dancing Lessons* with the social dancer in mind. Advertisements geared to vaudeville bookers claimed that it was cheaper for patrons to attend the film rather than to pay exhorbitant prices for dancing lessons. Said one advertisement: "Book this feature and you will show the greatest novelty since the invention of the motion pictures. It is something absolutely *new* and it actually teaches."[5] Ads and reviews of the film also appeared in dance periodicals such as *The Dancing Times*, which had a large readership of dance teachers. One can conjecture that these teachers may have picked up some tips from the movie, or that they may have urged their students to view it as a learning tool.

In using all of these materials, the researcher must continually weed out the purely promotional from "fact." Advertisements, of course, and even many of the newspaper and magazine features often contained inflated language and questionable dance descriptions. One way to determine the accuracy of these nontraditional sources is to compare them with descriptions from published dance manuals. As mentioned earlier, dance manuals of the period were usually written by professional dance teachers, and they offer the researcher the most reliable information about basic movement style and body positioning. Where possible, it is helpful to compare descriptions of the same dance from a variety of sources. For example, the look of the popular Aeroplane Waltz of 1914 became clear after consulting descriptions of the number in dance manuals, sheet music, newspaper features, and photographs. Ultimately, combining both traditional and non-traditional sources yields the truest picture of exhibition ballroom dance of the 1910s.

ENDNOTES

1 Irene and Vernon Castle, "New Dances for This Winter," *The Ladies' Home Journal*, ca, 1914 (Irene and Vernon Castle scrapbook, folder #1, Theatre Collection, The Museum of the City of New York).

2 Jose Collins, "The Latest Dances and How to Dance Them," 14 April, 1912 (Jose Collins scrapbook, NAFR #316, Robinson Locke Collection, The Billy Rose Theatre Collection, The New York Public Library).

3 "The Toddle Dance,' Joseph W. Stern & Co., 1916 (*MGZR, Toddle Dance, The Dance Collection, The New York Public Library).

4 Columbia double-disc records. Complete catalogue. November 1914, p. 146. (Rodgers and Hammerstein Archives of Recorded Sound, The New York Public Library.

5 Motion Picture Dancing Lessons, "Kalem Klip Sheet," *Kalem Kalendar*, 15 October 1913 (Kalem Company scrapbook, MFL n.c. 249, The Billy Rose Theatre Collection, The New York Public Library).

BIBLIOGRAPHY

'Buena Vista Tango.' Music by Louis Hirsch, pub: Shapiro, Bernstein & Co., Ltd., 1913.

Castle, Irene and Vernon. "New Dances for This Winter." *Ladies' Home Journal*, ca: 1914.

Castle, Mr. and Mrs. Vernon. *Modern Dancing*. New York: Harper and Bros., 1914.

Collins, Jose. "The Latest Dances and How to Dance Them." *The Louisville Herald*, April 1912.

Columbia double-disc records, Complete Catalogue, November 1914.

"The Dance Craze in Paris Creates New Types of Gowns." *Dress and Vanity Fair*, November 1913.

The Dolly Sisters. "Cuba Contributes to the Rumba." *The Newark Star Eagle*, 25 October 1915.

The Dolly Sisters. "Exhibition Dance of Year is Hindoo Moon: Described by Roszika Dolly." *The Newark Star Eagle*, 28 October 1916.

The Dolly Sisters. "Famous 'Dancing Dollies' Make Their Bow to Newarkers." *The Newark Star Eagle*, 23 October 1915.

The Dolly Sisters. "The Minuet Rag – A New Dance." *The Newark Star Eagle*, 26 October 1916.

The Dolly Sisters. " 'One-Step' Different This Year! Has Oriental Poses, Dollys Explain." *The Newark Star Eagle*, 27 October 1916.

Hallmark, Harrydele. "If You Dance You Must Pay the Piper." *Vogue*, 15 January 1914.

Inglis, William. "*Is Modern Dancing Indecent?*" Harper's Weekly, 17 May 1913.

"The Inner Circle Toddle," in 'The Toddle Dance.' Joseph W. Stein & Co., 1916.

'The Aeroplane Waltz,' (Joan Sawyer's New Dance Creation). Music by Charles Konedski-Davis, pub: Presto Publishing Co., 1914.

Kinney, Troy. "The New Dances, A Study of Art and Good Taste as Expressed in Modern Ballroom Dancing." *Woman's Home Companion*, October 1914.

Miller, Alice Duer. "The New Dances and the Younger Generation." *Harper's Bazaar*, May 1912.

'Modern Dances.' Music by Malvin Franklin, pub: Knickerbocker Music, 1914.

Motion Picture Dancing Lessons. "Kalem Klip Sheet," *Kalem Kalendar*. October 1913.

Mouvet, Maurice. *Maurice's Art of Dancing*. New York: G. Schirmer, 1915.

New Victor Records, Victor Records Monthly Catalogue. November 1914.

" 'Pivot Steps and Glides Chief Motions in Aeroplane Waltz,' says Joan Sawyer." Unidentified newspaper clipping, ca. 1914.

"The Turkey Trot, Grizzly Bear, and Other Naughty Diversions." *The New Bedford* (Connecticut) *Sunday Standard*, 4 February 1912.

'The Valse Hesitation, A Paraphrase on Dvorak's Humoresque.' Arranged by Ford T. Dabney, pub: Moffett Co., 1913.

Wilson, G. Hepburn. "Modern Dances are Not Vulgar." *The Modern Dance Magazine*, December/January 1917.

FASHION FILLERS IN SILENT FILM PERIODICALS

by Barbara Cohen-Stratyner

"Not only do the motion picture companies require their actresses to be garbed in the latest mode, but many of them are producing special films devoted to nothing but fashions. Sandwiched in between the smiles and tears of picture plays, [the smartly dressed woman] now sees the latest gowns almost as soon as they are turned out from the workshops of the designers. The popularity of the fashion display in films has not only added to the revenue of the picture palace proprietors, but has served to advertise the creators of fashion, for in all the special fashion films the name of the designer of the garments is always prominently displayed."
Moving Picture Publicity (July 1914)

The non-fiction film industry was not alone in its attempt to link the fashion-conscious consumer to its entertainment product. The film studios of the silent era introduced fashion parades into motion pictures. One studio based an entire serial on consumerism. Magazine publishing, a major subsidiary industry for the New York and Hollywood studios, also integrated fashion-consciousness into its many products. This article is a survey of the fashion information in the magazines that flourished in the silent film era.

BARBARA COHEN-STRATYNER is the Editor of *Performing Arts Resources* and Contributing Editor of *Contemporary Musicians*. A member of the faculty of the Parsons School of Design, she serves as Exhibition Curator for the Library & Museum for the Performing Arts, The New York Public Library. She has an M.F.A. in Design and a Ph.D. in Performance Studies — both from NYU.

As the silent film industry grew in the 1910s, studios and theatre owners developed media with which to catch and sustain its audience. Although moving pictures had been integrated almost completely into the American lifestyle, the art form was still young and many parts of the industry doubted its lasting ability to draw a paying audience. It became important for each studio to maintain its own corporate identity and to ensure that the audience did not stray to the product of its rival. Theater owners and touring exhibitors had to keep that audience from attending films at other places or returning to live entertainment forms. Most of the industry's efforts were directly at advertising and exploitation campaigns involving window cards, posters and gimmicks. But its leaders, many of whom had worked previously in other forms of entertainment, also turned to the standard literary forms of public contact – programs and magazines. Two forms of periodicals became popular – the house organ, which combined program information with exploitation materials, and the motion picture fan magazine.

Having based their periodicals on these theatrical models, the film studios and related industries adopted much of their style and content. House organs, published by the studios for the theatre owners, printed casts and scenarios along with offers of posters and lobby accessories. The fan monthlies and weeklies, like their models in theatre and lifestyle publications, combined prose scenarios with personality profiles and advice columns.

Both forms of film periodicals provide valuable information on the motion picture industry and product, of course. We can find scenarios, cast photographs, interviews with actors, directors and artisans for almost every film, as well as information on their advertising campaigns. But since the magazines were based on existing models from entertainment and general-interest publishing, they also contain tremendous stores of materials on related art forms, such as fashion, interior design, beauty and hygiene. This article, based on research at the Margaret Herrick Library, Academy of Motion Picture Arts and Sciences, and the Billy Rose Theatre Collection, The New York Public Library, covers only one of the lifestyle concerns that could be researched in the periodicals of the silent film era.

It is important to note that the fan magazines were often parts of chains of periodicals issued by a publisher. The film magazines could therefore rely on an existing subscription and advertising base. Many of the fan magazines also used the same writers and photographers as their company's theatre, fashion and general-interest publications. The finest photographers and illustrators could be employed by even the smallest film fan magazines since they were retained by related firms. Photographs by Arnold Genthe, best known for his images of Isadora Duncan, show "Our Mutual Girl" shopping in the weekly based on that serial. Illustrated articles about recent Paris and New York collections appeared very quickly in film fan magazines that were created by such general-interest publishing giants as Bernarr Mac-Fadden and Eugene V. Brewster.

The advertising base that these magazines inherited and shared relied on personal hygiene products and self-improvement mail-order courses. These provide contemporary researchers with a vital source of information about the wearers of fashion (and their shampoos, diets and dreams). They also provided the magazines with a degree of corporate freedom. With full color Palmolive ads in each issue, an editor was not dependent on advertising from film studios and could include more objective articles and reviews on individual motion pictures and performers.

For fashion historians and costume designers alike, the film magazines provide an invaluable source of text, photographs and illustrations. The clothing of the final fifteen years of the silent film era, 1914–1929, remain of enormous interest to us today. The first period, 1914–1919, saw the development of a general audience for couture and innovative retail clothing throughout the country. This period, although it seems to some to be reminiscent of the reliance on surface decoration of the nineteenth century, was one of the more experimental in the history of women's clothes. Designers in Paris, London and New York created collages of fabric and decorative elements in their attempts to perfect "impressionist" evening garments. For day and street wear, they developed new tailoring techniques that remain important in the garment industry today. Broadway producers and New York-based film studios purchased unique designs and ready-to-wear garments from the Fifth Avenue salons and retail stores that were favored by the social elite. Although some designers, most notably Lucy Sunderland, Lady Duff-Gordon (Lucile, Ltd.), were skilled at self-promotion, others relied on mentions in women's, fashion and entertainment magazines for name recognition. Some rarely documented French couturiers, such as Drécoll, are cited often in these film magazines. Retail outlets for clothing and accessories in a period in which no woman was seen on the streets without gloves and a hat also found the publicity value of descriptions and illustrations in the film magazines to be vital for their business success. We as 1989 historians are delighted that the magazines obliged since they often provide rare glimpses of garments attributed to their designers and stores, often with full descriptions and prices. Fashions of the 1920s are much better documented and have been more frequently studied, but film magazines offer unique sources of information here too. Both glamorous evening wear ("the Hollywood look") and street wear by Paris, London and New York designers are covered in the periodicals. One of the greatest values of this information is that it is monthly and the minute variations of fashion in hemlines, trimmings, silhouettes and style can be seen as a slow evolution. An interview with a fashionably dressed actress in December 1922 that reveals her delighted that long skirts are back is important evidence that the flapper look was not universally admired by the young and glamorous. It should be remembered that film-promoted clothing did not necessarily follow our views of 1920s style. I could find no references in the surveyed magazines to clothing by Chanel or Lanvin although those two designers, now recognized as the most creative of the decade, were frequently cited in the theatre-based magazines of the era. Some designers, however, are surprisingly well documented in the film magazines. Lucien Lelong, who was not discovered by the general fashion-conscious public until the mid-1930s, was featured in a double-page spread in *Movie Magazine* in 1926 and cited in *Moving Picture Stories* as early as 1923.

Film magazines can be divided into these periodicals aimed at the public and those "house organs" whose targeted audiences are the theatre owners, booking agents and managers. These magazines, published by the studios or distribution houses, were created as advertising media catalogues for individual films and serials. They provided a continuing file of scenarios and cast lists of available films for the theatre managers. The weekly magazines, which were mailed a month before the film was scheduled for distribution, also included promotional information on films and performers, advertisements for studio-produced items, such as the 17 foot "curtain call films" produced by Kalem for its 1914 serials, and samples of articles suitable for local newspapers. Replicas of posters, one-, three-and six-sheets, and other items designed for theatre lobbies were published, often in color.

Fashion information in house organs was generally limited to the sample newspaper and program announcements. Occasionally, promotional items were provided with captions that identified colors and fabric. One of the most informative items in a studio organ identified a garment's designer as the innovative New York-based couturiere Lucile, Ltd. As often occurred with

Lucile, Ltd., the price was cited as a feature of the garment. It was a full page offer for "a splendid attraction for your lobby . . . an almost life-size" oil portrait of Kalem star Alice Joyce from the final page of the December 1, 1914 *Kalem Kalendar*. The advertisement specified that "this painting shows Miss Joyce as she appears in *The Theft of the Crown Jewels*," in which she wears a $3000 Lucile (Lady Duff-Gordon) gown and $1,000,000 in genuine jewelry furnished by Lebolt & Co., of Fifth Avenue, New York."

Paramount Studios published a variety of house organs as well as magazines aimed at both exhibitors and the public. *Paramount Magazine* (December 1914–June 1915) and Paramount's *Picture Progress* (July 1915–December 1916) both featured a fashion column in each issue. Throughout the short life of *Paramount Magazine* and for the first six issues of *Picture Progress*, the illustrated articles were concerned only with contemporary street fashion. The first, "My Lady's Boudoir: Some Smart Suggestions from Paris," a holiday guide to gift items, was unsigned, but most of the columns were by fashion journalists Helen Vivian Lightfoot or Mary Ripley. Their articles included photographs of 2–4 outfits, identified by designer and/or retail source, and, as can be seen, were extremely detailed.

". . . These charming slippers are ornamented with a small buckle of silver set with rhinestones, while two silver chains fasten across the instep, ending in small round ornaments from which hang rhinestones, These slippers, as can be seen, are immensely chic when worn with sheer silk stockings which are embroidered in white silk." "Some Smart Suggestions from Paris" (December, 1914)

". . . This hat, in one of the newest shapes, is of tête de nègre brown velvet. The crown is very full and soft, fitting well down over the head. Across the front is placed diagonally a most unusual fantasie of cock's feathers which, instead of curling naturally, is wired to lie flat. These are in the natural colors of dark green, and in the center is a feather ornament of black. Worn with one of the new, close-fitting fur neckpieces, this hat is distinguished and very smart." "My Lady's Boudoir: Winter Hats That Have Style and Distinction" (January 1915)

". . . The gown shown in the illustration is of fine white batiste with a deep flounce of cut-out embroidery over a plain petticoat of filet lace. The waist is made in blouse fashion, trimmed with two bands of the embroidery, and a note of color is given by a very wide girdle of mustard-colored satin trimmed with two rows of blue moire silk ribbon – a very French touch! The hat worn with this costume has a crown of black satin covered with black tulle and the transparent brim is of tulle ornamented with one large yellowish pink rose. The parasol is of white linen with eyelet embroidery." "Charming Summer Fashions" (July 1915)

". . . This suit is of midnight blue serge, the coat, large patch pockets and tabs, which are inserted in the underarm seam at the back, are bound with black half-inch silk braid, and a black velvet collar adds a touch of character which otherwise might be lacking. The skirt is circular, fitting closely around the hips and falling in graceful lines at the bottom. For a general utility suit, combining smartness and economy, no better choice could be made." "Staple Fashions for the Fall" (October 1915)

From December 1915 on, the column shifted to a purely promotional focus. Cynthia Marlowe interviewed Pauline Frederick in her "Bella Donna Gowns" in that issue. The four photographed gowns are described by both women: " 'Iris, that black Drécoll gown, please! I'm sure you'll say it can't be improved upon!' It was black tulle, a veritable dream, standing out very full at the hips with rows of black satin-ribbon pump bows, set vertically above tulle plaitings, a decidedly new trimming; the bodice decorated with a silver-embroidered ceinture." A double page spread in the November 1916 issue focused on the dance frocks promoted by Florence Walton (of the exhibition ballroom team of Maurice and Walton). Six frocks are described and illustrated with photographs, among them, "this dress . . . of flesh colored tulle with ruffles of blue tulle edged in the same colored silk. Festoons of hand-made roses in pale shades are draped around skirt and over one side of bodice. The under-skirt is of sequin Bisson embroidery. The bodice is trimmed with the same embroidery."

For 1916, *Picture Progress* switched to promoting clothing specific to Paramount films. The garments were designed and the articles were written and illustrated by S. Zalud, a Broadway-based costumer working concurrently for Paramount's New York Studios and the Shubert Brothers' Winter Garden Theater. The fashion-journalist-style articles predict trends with accuracy and detail, but neither the films or the performers are identified in Zalud's articles. *Picture Progress* then switched to a new column – "On The Avenue: seen and sketched by Marjorie Mouat." Mouat's style combined explicit fashion description with name dropping, as in this December 1916 article:

"I caught Blanche Sweet hurrying into the elevator of the building at Fifth Avenue and Forty-First Street that houses the Famous Players-Lasky-Paramount offices and managed to retain an indelible impression of her hat before she vanished from sight. This dashing *chapeau* was made of silk beaver, faced with rows on rows of Grosgrain ribbon. A glossy plush crown was set in the mesh of shining silk, like the center of a black-eyes Susan. This unique hat was as perfect a match for Miss Sweet's personality as is her manner."

Magazines aimed at the film-going public were based on the models of popular general-interest monthlies. Like *Ladies' Home Journal* or *Physical Culture*, they included a range of fashion-oriented articles. Some were information pieces on that classic early 20th century American trinity of health, beauty and independence, as endorsed by MacFadden, Curtis and Hearst publications. Others promoted individual films or their stars through interviews and photographs of costumes or personal garments. A survey of film fan and general interest magazines in the holdings of the Billy Rose Theatre Collection, The New York Public Library, and the Margaret Herrick Library, the Academy of Motion Picture Arts and Sciences, show that most of the magazines varied their styles of fashion reporting during their lives. Five magazines that among them cover the 1914–1929 era have been selected to demonstrate the range of articles between the mid-1910s and the end of the silent film era.

Motion Picture Classics, in its first fashion column, November 1915, focused on the garments themselves, with an uncredited photograph and description layout that imitated those in *Vogue*: "Exclusive Up-to-the Minute Fashions Direct from Paris for Supplement Readers." Descriptions were explicit, among them, "One of the smart suits recently imported is shown in navy blue duyveteen featuring a flaring skirt and coat. The marked severeness and simplicity of this garment is broken only by the deep band of black seal fur which is evident on the flare of the coat, high collar and cuffs. Smart button boots and a trim velvet hat with saucy chin strap complete the outfit."

By the next issue, the wearers, not the gowns, became the centers of attention. Mabel Warren was credited with the text which featured photographs of contemporary film actresses. The descriptions are much less detailed, substituting complimentary adjectives for color and textile information, for example, "Mary

Fuller is shown in a stunning costume of cloth with collars and cuffs of fur. Fancy buttons are introduced in the gown."

In early volumes of *Photo-Play Journal*, textual articles analyzing the clothing theories of both performers and studio staff designers were featured. In September 1918, Pearl Gaddis interviewed Balboa Studio's "Sun-kist Star," actress Jacqueline Saunders while they shopped at Harry Collins in New York. Between praise for Saunders' garden in Hollywood and of her menu at tea, Gaddis described four outfits by Collins, including his "evening frock of American Beauty velvet . . . made with a lovely, sweeping train and with wide-open, very long angel-sleeves of silvery net, while the skirt, in front, was looped up over an embroidered petticoat of silver net." Two months later, *Photo-Play Journal* ran an uncredited interview with Cecil B. DeMille about his selection of clothes for film use; it featured a photograph of Alpharetta Hoffman, staff designer for Lasky Studio, but did not quote her. Also in that November 1918 issue was Adele Whitely Fletcher's "Fine Feathers" which claimed that "Once upon a time the venerable person, Dame Fashion, had her abode in gay Paree. But when that spectre-like thing Germany's mailed fist, threatened to crush the European continent, she changed her residence to New York, U.S.A., where she now rules supreme." Fletcher described the American-designed garments worn by seven film actresses and the ballroom team of Jansci and Roszika Dolly. She balanced promotional text with descriptions, as in "Mae Allison, who has made many Metro productions delightful through her dainty clothes, declares that never before did she find such a pretty afternoon frock as this one of silver grey chiffon over coral silk. The girdle is embroidered in pearl and coral beads, while the narrow bands of soft grey squirrel conform beautifully with the exquisite coloring of the frock itself." Unfortunately, Fletcher does not identify any of the American designers by name.

Photoplay Magazine, the classic fan magazine that lasted until 1980, ran periodic fashion columns throughout its existence. In the mid-1910s, "The National Movie Publication" relied on columnist Lillian Howard to provide 3–5 page articles with photographs that focused on a single actress. In January 1916, for example, she contributed "Adorning a Dawn" (about New York-based Hazel Dawn of Famous Players) with descriptions of Dawn's career, her family farm, her politics (Suffragist) and wardrobe. Howard identified the sources of the illustrated garments, which include rare examples of the work of retail designers Giddings and Hickson. In the next issue, Howard related Marguerite Courtot's dress reform-inspired theories of appropriate clothes in the coyly-titled "How I Teach My Gowns to Act." This article, and Howard's "Genevieve, Your Stockings" (May 1916), are invaluable guides for the color schemes of clothing in film. Courtot described the rules of color in black and white filming:

> ". . . There is no color in the photographed gown, yet through tone values different colors in the same gown do seem to exist on the screen. I must help the lens of the camera by considering how various tints and shades will register. a coral hue of pink will come out as dark as a mouse gray, even darker if the gray be a silky velvet with a sheen to it . . . For white, I use a gown of pale yellow, delicate blue or pink. White itself would come up glaring and hard, cutting out instead of softening into a contrasting background. If the effect of a black gown is desired, I select one in purple which, because of the red in it, comes out in the pictures a deep rich black, whereas actual black would appear rusty and dull."

In June 1920, *Photoplay Magazine* announced the appointment of actress Constance Talmadge as its fashion columnist, cited her as "the screen's best-dressed star." Her columns analyzed trends in couture design, without reference to films. Her first column referred to historical influences on Jean Patou and Agnès [Grès] and traced the past uses of the redingote silhouette and the basque bodice. By late 1922, the magazine had combined its fashion and advice pages under the egis of columnist Carolyn Van Wyck and her "Department of Personal Service." *Photoplay* offered patterns based on the wardrobe of film actress in Winter 1922/1923. In the December issue, for example, Van Wyck's page featured a short interview with Alice Terry, and captioned sketches for a street dress and dinner dress. Each had detailed descriptions and estimates of fabric quantities and prices. The fashion spreads were almost completely pictorial, focusing on garments worn in specific films or by well known actresses. Descriptions were detailed and, when the film title was not named, information about the designer or source was often given fully. For example, in the March 1923 four-page "The Spring Gowns, from Paris and New York via the Photoplay, sound note of classic simplicity," 11 photographs of Bebe Daniels, Hedda Hopper and Andree Lafayette and four line drawings traced the Paris and New York collections from street wear through to evening wraps. They include the following descriptions of unusual creations by important couturieres:

"Paris incarnate. The keynote of Andrée Lafayette's every gown. This, by Madeleine Vionnet, is of white crepe de chine embroidered in silver. With a pointed hemline, a train and a garland of large flat roses banding the hips."

"Another of the Andrée Lafayette frocks. A delicate, cobwebby dress — created by Jenny from white georgette crepe which falls, in classic Greek lines, over a foundation of ivory satin. The edges are embroidered in tiny crystal beads, the hemline is decidedly uneven, and — there is only one sleeve!"

The long-lived *Picture-Play Magazine* published a wide range of fashion articles. In November 1917, at the height of the exhibition ballroom era, it ran an interview by Tarleton Winchester of Mrs. Vernon Castle. "A Conference on Clothes" was exceedingly general and, although it included three full-length portraits of Castle in gowns that she had designed, they are not described. In the early 1920s, *Picture-Play Magazine* ran a double-page illustrated column by Louise Williams that combined general beauty advice with descriptions of photographed garments as worn by the promoted actresses. In "Frocks That Say Something," in October 1921, she warned her readers against outfits that didn't "jell" and recommended that they look to Betty Compson for examples: "Let's consider the costume which Miss Compson wears in the first photograph on this page . . . See how well it balances. The drapery of the frock extends on one side; the feathers of the hat on the other. Her white collar and cuffs are supplemented by her white gloves. The necessary note of color is introduced in the knot of flowers at her waist and in the bead bag. There is perfect simplicity and there is harmony of line and effort — and in just such little, subtle touches lies the secret of being beautifully dressed." In December 1921, Williams answered the question "What's Your Texture" with examples from Priscilla Dean, Miss Dupont ("whom you have seen in Universal Pictures") and Lillian Gish.

As *Picture-Play Magazine* became larger and more profusely illustrated in the later 1920s, it ran more fashion and beauty articles in each issue. Some were purely illustrative, such as "Speaking of Chic," in December 1927, which showed five photographs of Mary Astor with captions ranging from dressmaker detail ("an afternoon frock of heavy, black figured satin, embellished with a cream-colored jabot") to advertising slogans ("The wedding gown worn by Miss Astor, above, is fashion's latest decree, and is as patrician as the beauty of its wearer"). Other articles gave general beauty advice using film actresses as examples. Vera Standing's

"A Short Cut to Beauty," in that issue, explained how different hairdo's brought out the beauty of specific stars, among them, Greta Garbo, Norma Shearer, Lois Moran and Billie Dove. The latter actress was given compliments, promotion, and advice in Standing's descriptions – "in *The Black Pirate*, where she was conventionally beautiful, and in *The Stolen Bride*, where she was breath-taking," due to her changing bangs.

The rival *Moving Picture Stories* featured fashion and beauty advice columns written by (or at least credited to) film actresses. They promoted the performers as ideal American women – active, energetic and eager to make the most out of their natural resources. Exercise was recommended at all times, even in columns about fashion, such as Norma Talmadge's "The Summer Girl and Her Clothes" in the June 23, 1922 issue. *Moving Picture Stories* ran a four-part series, "Keeping Fit with Doris Kenyon," from January 5 – January 26, 1923, in which that actress promoted walking and posed for a two-page spread of calisthenics in a middy blouse and bloomers.

The magazine ran fashion advice articles by Marion Davies and Constance Talmadge, who recommended a evening wrap by famed couturier Lucien Lelong, "which I am wearing in my latest First National attraction, *Dangerous Business.*" Davies described her period costumes for *When Knighthood Was in Flower* as well as contemporary street clothes in her column, "What the Blonde Should Wear," in January 5, 1923. Her explicit descriptions of both includes a recommendation of suitable colors that she wore "even if the camera cannot record them."

Moving Picture Stories also ran advice columns from celebrities concerning personal hygiene – a subject usually left for euphemistic advertisements. In the January 5, 1923 issue, for example, Ethel Clayton wrote her advice on "Why Hairs Go Wrong," recommending scalp massage and one hundred strokes of brushing a day. In the next issue, on January 12, the readers could learn "Why Teeth Leave Home" from Pearl White.

Movie Magazine was one of the few general-interest periodical that did not publish scenarios or plot abstracts. It aimed at film fans with a combination of personality profiles, photo-layouts, serialized fiction set in Hollywood, and gossip. That the latter was written after the regular columns can be readily seen in the contents of the October 1925 issue, which featured "Dinner with the Valentinos (And the Menu and Recipes Which Made the Dinner a Success)" on page 49 and "Why the Valentinos Separated" on page 58. *Movie Magazine* featured at least one fashion column and one interior decor article per issue in its early volumes. In that October's issue, Charles D. Chapman (Interior Decorator [i. e. Art director] for Famous-Players Laskey) explained "What to do About the Windows" while Cerline Boll "Let the Screen Bring Paris to Your Front Door." After February 1926, the editors added a continuing series of articles by Perry Westmore on make-up and beauty.

In Boll's column, she recommended ways to adapt contemporary fashions from film into street clothes for the modest income level. In October, she gave advice about an evening wrap worn by Constance Talmadge in *Her Sister from Paris*: ". . . a coat-type wrap of crepe Roma. It is white with wide bands and lining of vermilion. It is a gracefully beautiful thing, subdued with silver embroidery and bordered with white fox. It might easily be made of velvet. Then bands of fur about the bottom and the sleeves could be used. No embroidery would be necessary." Most of Boll's columns featured five or more garments as worn by different actresses in their current films. Occassionally, she focused on a single performer or couturier, as in her February 1926 article "Select Clothes That Look Well in Movement," which focused on garments designed by Lucien Lelong for Gilda Gray's personal wardrobe. Boll's illustrations and descriptions make her columns invaluable for both fashion historians and costume designers since she detailed colors, textiles and accessories, as in this May 1926 article, "There is Never a Luxury Tax on Good Taste:"

> "This costume has become almost a uniform for the smartest women in both New York and Paris. The cape-coat is made of navy blue reps, but blues of every shade are worn, although the darker ones are more practical. It is lined with black satin and can be worn open as in the illustration or wrapped about. The dress Corinne Griffith wears [from *Mille. Modiste*] illustrates a slight change in the silhouette by the introduction of a black leather belt, full pleated skirt, and for added chic and individuality, a long silver chain with very large links. She wisely wears 'Peel' oxfords with flat heels and simple felt hat."

Although many filmed fashion shows were integrated into plotted movies or distributed as newsreels in the first decades of the silent film era, there was only one long-running serial created purely to feature contemporary clothing. This consumerist cliffhanger was *Our Mutual Girl*, distributed by the Reliance Motion Picture Company in 1914 and 1915. The serial ran through three stories about "Margaret," a poor girl from the country who was adopted and given a debutante season by her indulgent rich aunt in New York. The films followed her through her days of shopping and escaping from villains. Unlike the suspense plots by Irwin Cobb and Albert Le Vino, which were non-realistic, the life style that was portrayed for her involved actual people and stores. The imaginary "Margaret" and her real-life companion, artist Jean Parke, were seen visiting such world-famous figures as Andrew Carnegie and Walter Damrosch, and visiting such well-known stores as Franklyn Simon. Because the stories were written around their commercial sponsorships, the plots cannot stand up to competition from Pearl White. Unlike "Pauline," "Margaret" took shopping more seriously than perils – she found an abandoned baby in one episode and bought her a layette before reporting to the police.

After reel 18, Reliance published a free magazine, *Our Mutual Girl Weekly*, that was distributed at the theatres that showed the serial. Subtitled, "A Magazine of People and Places, Fads and Fashions," it concentrated on "Margaret's" chief concern – clothing. Because of the serial's concern with retail stores rather than individual designers (who would have been less likely to donate garments and salon facilities), the fashion reportage in the magazine focuses on purchasable garments for street wear by the typical young woman of the audience. This makes it a valuable source of fashion advice for the normal American of what is now known as the Junior market.

A typical issue of this short-lived magazine included a column by its editor or by the president of the film corporation; an analysis of the plot so far and the week's reel; a double spread of photographs and a page of short blurbs on "People and Places" visited by "Margaret" (featuring working women, such as the New York Commissioner of Corrections); a beauty and health column; a "Dear Girl Friends" letter from "Margaret;" and at least two fashion pages. The descriptions were exceedingly detailed and give information about fabric, color, care and design; a page of accessories was also included in many issues. The targeted market of the film remained the focus of the fashion pages as well unlike most fan magazines which presented glamorous clothing. *Our Mutual Girl Weekly* promoted clothing suitable for a young working woman of the era – tailored suits, shirtwaists and skirts. Additional fashion information is given in the magazine on the final page which featured an advertisement for May Manton Patterns, offered free with an Our Mutual Girl coupon.

There is little question that this information can be of great interest and value to fashion historians and costumers, but it can also be of value to many social historians. The image of the American woman as promoted in the fashion filler columns of film magazines was related to that created by the motion pictures themselves, but it was not identical. The ability of the film industry to adapt its products to variations in its market—those who buy tickets vs those who buy magazines—is worth a study in itself. Fashion, unlike more ephemeral concepts as self-image, can be analyzed as a commodity and as a vocabulary that spreads and contracts within a public. The film magazine fashion columns are as valuable a source for garment information as those in theatre or women's periodicals. Since we know that the targeted markets for *Photoplay, Movie* and *Our Mutual Girl* were different, we can learn how garments from the silent film era, 1914–1929, were created for these consumer audiences.

The magazines themselves are available in full (or almost complete) runs only in the major centers of film research, but single issues can be found in many university and historical society libraries. It is unfortunate that most of the magazines were printed on self-destructing paper and that few, if any, spines are extant. However, more and more are becoming available on microfilm, and, despite the difficulties of using visual materials in that medium, they are being preserved.

Bibliographic Guides to Film Periodicals:

Brady, Anna, Richard Wall and Carolynn N. Weiner. *Union List of Film Periodicals. Holdings of Selected American Collections.* Westport, Connecticut: Greenwood Press, 1984.

Gilbert, Basil. "Film Periodicals – a Historical Survey, Part I – United States." *Cinema Papers*, No.14 (October 1977), pp 142–143, 187.

Slide, Anthony, ed. *International Film, Radio and Television Journals.* Westport, Connecticut: Greenwood Press, 1985.

Film Periodicals Cited:

Complete or partial runs at the Margaret Herrick Library, Academy of Motion Picture Arts and Sciences (AMPAS) and at the Billy Rose Theatre Collection, The New York Public Library (BRTC).

Kalem Kalendar.
January 1913–December 1915. Issued to coincide with release schedule. Published by the Kalem Film Corporation, New York City. AMPAS, BRTC.

Motion Picture Classic. [Motion Picture Classic and Supplement]
September 1915–August 1931. Monthly. Published by Eugene V. Brewster, Brooklyn, New York. AMPAS, BRTC, Museum of Modern Art Film Library.

Movie Magazine.
March 1915–December 1915. Monthly. Published by Movie Magazine Company, Los Angeles. BRTC.

Moving Picture Publicity.
December 1913–July 1914. Monthly. Published by the T & C Publicity Co., New York. BRTC.

Moving Picture Stories.
January 3, 1913–October 29, 1929. Weekly. Published by Harry E. Wolff, New York. AMPAS, BRTC, Museum of Modern Art Film Library.

Our Mutual Girl Weekly. [Film]
1914–1915. Issued to coincide with release of each reel. Published by the Reliance Motion Picture Corporation, New York. BRTC.

Paramount Magazine / Picture Progress.
December 3, 1914–November 22, 1917. Weekly. Published by Paramount Pictures, New York. AMPAS, BRTC.

Picture-Play Magazine. [*Picture Play* (1941); *Charm* (1957)]
April 10, 1915–February, 1927. Monthly. Published by Street & Smith, New York. BRTC, Museum of Modern Art Film Library.

Photo Play.
August 1911–December 1941. Monthly. [after merge with *Movie Mirror*, continued publication until May/June 1980]. Published by the Photoplay Magazine Publishing Co., Chicago [MacFadden Publishing Company]. AMPAS (card index available), BRTC, Museum of Modern Art Film Library. Available on University Microfilm, Ann Arbor, Michigan.

Photo-Play Journal.
May 1916–February 1921. Monthly. Published by the Central Press Company, Philadelphia. AMPAS, BRTC.